FACING

SOCIAL REVOLUTION

FACING SOCIAL REVOLUTION:

The Personal Journey of a Quaker Economist

by Jack Powelson
with a Foreword by Jim Corbett
and an Afterword by Kenneth Boulding

HORIZON SOCIETY PUBLICATIONS
BOULDER COLORADO
in cooperation with the Social Order Series of
The Pacific Yearly Meeting of the
Religious Society of Friends

Second Edition,

Published by Horizon Society Publications, 45 Bellevue Dr., Boulder CO 80302, in cooperation with the Social Order Series of the Pacific Yearly Meeting of the Religious Society of Friends.

PRINTED IN THE UNITED STATES OF AMERICA.

Library of Congress Cataloging-in-Publication Data

Powelson, John P., 1920-
Facing Social Revolution

Bibliography:p.
Includes index.

1. Powelson. John P., 1920- . 2. Economists—United States—Biography. 3. Quakers—United States—Biography. I. Title.
HB119.P68A3 1987 330'.092'4 [B] 86-32186
ISBN 0-9618242-0-4

In Memoriam

JACK GILMORE

TABLE OF CONTENTS

FOREWORD

by Jim Corbett
Pima Meeting (Tucson AZ), and Sanctuary

Facing Social Revolution sets forth the basic choices confronting those who would serve love rather than violence. Extensive experience, painstaking study, unflinching honesty, and clear Quaker insight underpin Jack Powelson's challenge to the current commonplaces of coercion. His plain speech about war's new clothes is particularly refreshing, in view of the reluctance of Quakers to question the validity of the latest "just war" mythology.

And now that he mentions it, doesn't the newest champion look remarkably like old Moloch,* once again masquerading as a fashionable cause? Whatever revolutionary new styles it assumes, "just war" morality still cloaks the rule of violence.

If I were asked to recommend to Quakers a single title for social concerns discussion groups, this book would be it. Our peace testimony is at issue.

---

*Moloch, or Molech, a deity to whom child sacrifices were offered by the Israelites in the days of the monarchy (Encyclopedia Britannica, 1974: Micropedia vol. VI, p. 982).

PREFACE

This book arises from a sense of compulsion, even duty, to set forth the tortuous path of intellectual and religious searching for the Truth which I have traveled as Quaker, pacifist, and economist. The path has been beset with doubts, confusion, error, hard work, and gratifying illuminations.

It is a personal journey in two senses. Part One is my journey through professional assignments in the Third World: the people I have met and what we said to each other - in government, in the universities, in a land invasion, and in the slums. Part Two is my journey through history, trying to sense the meaning of what I had experienced. Inspiring me in both parts is the Society of Friends, with whose members I have shared many of my feelings. But this book is intended for others of similar mind as well as for Quakers. Much of it is about why I wrote it.

After desert-like years of uncertainty and search, both insights and continuing questions have sprung forth. Perhaps together we can face the problem: How can the values Quakers hold dear be affirmed in these times of great social revolution?

Jack Powelson

ACKNOWLEDGMENTS

In my own Friends Meeting, in Boulder, Colorado, it has been customary for any member to ask for a "clearness committee," similar to those for membership and marriage, to counsel on any important, pending decision. I asked for a clearness committee to advise me on this book. Martin Cobin, clerk; Dick Counihan, convener; Mary Hey, Judith Howell, Jerry Krenz, Med Medrud, Connie Sawyer, Steve Thomas, and Wolf Thron were appointed by the monthly business meeting. They read the manuscript, sat twice by themselves and once with me, then reported back to the meeting.

During a visit in Philadelphia, I lunched with Asia Bennett and Joe Volk of the American Friends Service Committee and asked for a similar clearness committee of AFSC staff. This was arranged; the committee read the draft manuscript; and on a later occasion I met with them: Warren Witte, convener, and Judy Claude, Tom Conrad, Dave Elder, Corinne Johnson, Mohulatsi Mokeyame, and Joe Volk.

In addition, forty-one Friends-at-large read the manuscript and made comments. These were Steve Angell, Martha Avery, Lloyd Bailey, Hugh Barbour, Kitty Barragato, Elise and Kenneth Boulding, Edwin Bronner, Paul Carlson, Josephine Coats, Linda Coffin, Jim and Pat Corbett, Hugh Davidson, Dave Edinger, Chuck Fager, Herb and Mandy Fraser, Nelson and Marian Fuson, Pat and Jack Gilmore, Barbara Greenler, Barry Hollister, Paul Johnson, Stan Marshall, Tom Moore, Dave Mueller, Norma Price, Bob Schutz, Dan Seeger, Maia Soper, Allen Stokes, Bruce Thron-Weber, Thomas Todd, Brinton Turkle, Carol Urner, Bob Vogel, J.D. Von Pischke, Gilbert White, and Elaine Yarbrough. Tracy Mott, a colleague in economics, also read the manuscript and offered suggestions.

Members of my own family offered encouragement and advice. My wife, Robin Powelson, read every draft. Each time, her comments helped shape the next one. Constructive advice also came from our five children: Cynthia Powelson, Judith Powelson, Kenneth Powelson, Carolyn Powelson, Lawrence Powelson; and from my sister, Louise Powelson Dudley.

Traditionally, Friends have traveled to each other's meetings to express concerns. This book comes in the nature of a concern. Recognizing this, the Friends World Committee for Consultation has given me permission to use its mailing list to contact Friends' meetings to tell of this book. I am indebted to Gordon Browne and Anne Moore for arranging this and especially to Anne for sending me the up-to-date list.

I am indebted to my student assistants, Pam Killiany and Katherine Tokarsky, for typing and indexing, and to Peter Forsyth of Desktop Publishing and Liz deCaracena of Business Express for the physical production of the book.

In questioning my accuracy, my manner of presentation, my interpretation of information, and my selection of ideas, both the clearness committees, the Friends-at-large, and my own family offered invaluable help. While many revisions resulted from their inputs, I take full responsibility for the final product.

PART ONE

JOURNEY IN THE THIRD WORLD

Chapter 1

My Confession

My professional life was in turmoil in 1973. For twenty-five years, it had been divided between university teaching on the one hand and consulting and lecturing in the Third World on the other. In that year, I decided that much of what I was teaching, saying, and doing was wrong.

This insight did not come upon me suddenly. I had begun to suspect it years before I took action. But one day something snapped. I was sitting in the office of the Minister of Finance of Kenya.

I had been sent to Kenya by the Ford Foundation to help write the five-year economic plan. The Foundation had insisted - and I had eagerly agreed - that I would work for the Kenyans. They were my bosses, and I would be the faithful employee. I sat in on meetings between high government officials and corporate officers of multinationals. There I became convinced that the government officials, not the multinationals, were in charge. I examined agricultural plans and road-building plans; I helped decide how much to ask from the World Bank and how the proceeds would be spent. I argued for more aid to small farmers and less for a modern highway system, and I lost. I argued for family planning and listened to the guffaws of Ministry experts who joked about how they would not sell condoms without giving demonstrations.

The breaking point came on the interest rate. I was asked to write the five-year-plan chapter on fiscal and monetary policy. That meant projecting the government budget. My Kenyan counterpart, who was supposed to work with me, was not interested. I suspected he knew the plan was not to be taken seriously. So I did it all myself. When I came to the paragraph on the interest rate, I went counter to earlier plans. Previously, the rate had been kept artificially low, so that "economic development would be encouraged through easy access to credit." I knew that was a euphemism for rich people with connections borrowing scarce capital cheaply. They had a history of using borrowed capital for tourist hotels more than for helping the poor.

In the Third World, where the scarce supply of capital may drive up the market interest rate - often to 20% or more - the authorities frequently keep it artificially low, say 5% or less - a difference of fifteen points or more. The demand for such cheap credit is so great that if all potential borrowers were satisfied, the increase in money would be highly inflationary. Typically, therefore, the authorities ration credit to themselves, to their friends, and to rich farmers. So none is left for small farmers or tiny family businesses at any interest rate.

So, entirely on my own initiative, I wrote that over the next five years interest rates would be held high, "to reflect the scarcity of capital" and to promote employment. Hiring people would then be more attractive than using interest-costly machines. But the Permanent Secretary, to whom I reported, would have none of it. "Go back and write it over," he said, "with low interest rates."

The impossible choice I had both dreaded and predicted was now upon me. If I wrote "low interest rates," then I would connive in robbing the poor. If I wrote "high interest rates," I would disobey the boss I had promised to serve. If I did nothing, I would be derelict.

I decided the third choice was the least offensive. So I returned the draft to the Permanent Secretary with no change.

I appended a note, saying why, and that if he wanted "low interest rates" he would have to ask one of his Kenyan economists to write it. Then I waited.

A week later I was summoned to the office of the Minister of Finance. The top-level planning team was there, about five of us. Lo and behold! The minister held the chapter I had submitted to the Permanent Secretary, even though chapters were not supposed to go to him until the Permanent Secretary had approved. It turned out that the Permanent Secretary had been out of town. The Minister did not want to wait, so he would just skip the prior approval.

The meeting was conducted in the manner of all meetings I had attended with high officials in Kenya and in other less developed countries. The Minister was the only one who spoke. He stated what he liked about the chapter, and if there was anything to change he would order it done. He asked no questions, and those present knew better than to express opinions. We were there to hear and obey, not to draw on our expertise. Finally he said, "I like this chapter. It is approved."

So I faced a new dilemma. If I spoke up, I would be questioning the Minister, which simply "wasn't done." If I did not, I would face the wrath of the Permanent Secretary, for letting the Minister approve a chapter that had contravened his instructions. Finally I said, "Mr. Minister, in all due respect, I believe you should know that this chapter contains a paragraph that your Permanent Secretary does not approve."

"What? How can that be?," he asked, flabbergasted. I pointed to the paragraph and explained the circumstances. The Minister read it quickly. "Sounds fine to me," he said. "The chapter is approved."

Had I won a victory over the Permanent Secretary? Of course not. I knew the plan was an empty exercise. No matter what it said, there would be low interest rates. All I had done was to keep from participating in the conspiracy myself. I waited for the anger of the Permanent Secretary, but it did not come. After all, the Minister had knowingly approved the chapter, and questioning the Minister "isn't done."

If the plan was an empty exercise, so also were my two years writing it, except to contribute to my own education. Experiences such as this - some of which I will tell in subsequent chapters - gradually had led me to believe third-world governments were far more opportunistic, far more greedy, far more authoritarian, than I had ever imagined. As we lobby for foreign aid or argue for new international economic orders or want higher prices for third-world exports or ask to forgive the debts of rich people in poor countries, are we aware of how much we would deliver to greedy, dishonest politicians, and how they would use their new money-power to extract even more from the poor?

Chapter 2

Quiet and Reflection

So my career silently changed. Upon returning to the University of Colorado, I began to reflect and to read history. I wanted to know what really caused some areas of the world to become better able, and more willing, to attend to their poor than others. I no longer trusted modern economics, which led to planning and government action. I wanted to find out how it had happened in the past.

For five years I did little else than teach my courses and read history. No more foreign assignments. My publishing output plummeted, and I might have "perished" had I not had tenure. I did co-author two books, however: one a textbook on economic development, which did not sell very well, possibly because it criticized mainstream economics; the other a critique of the New International Economic Order, which got me into trouble with a lot of Quakers.

As I read histories of China, the Middle East, Africa, Latin America, and Europe, I began to teach courses in economic history rather than economic development. If there was any answer, I thought, it lay in history. How could I find it? It wasn't set forth in any one place. So I read widely, and every time I came upon something that related to economic development, or poverty versus wealth, I would jot it down, with its source, on a 3x5 index card. After five years, I had thousands of these cards. Now, after thirteen years, I have over ten thousand examples, all classified and in my computer.

Only after five years did I begin to tell others what I was doing. In my profession, frivolity is frowned on, and I did not want my colleagues to know I was learning things that others had written rather than myself pushing the edges of knowledge. But after five years, I began to see a pattern to my historical search. I began to think maybe I was on the track of why Europe and Japan were leaders in economic development, and why Asia, Latin America, and Africa were so far behind.

My new book would be called *The Horizon Society: An Historical Theory of Economic Development*. It is not yet written; it may be ten years away right now. Why the "horizon" society rather than the "ultimate" society? My colleagues of a century and a half ago used to write about the "stationary state" - the "end-economy" we were being led to - that John Stuart Mill thought would be much better than the present state. But I cannot imagine social evolution coming to an end. The horizon society is only as far as we can see.

So I tried to think of the kind of world I would like to live in. Peace, justice, conflict-resolution, love, all seemed part of economic development. My professional career and my Quaker career began to merge. But how could I talk of love with my colleagues in economics? How could I talk of economics with Quakers? I faced the conflict to which Kenneth Boulding refers in his Afterword to this book.

I would write an *institutional* theory. For Quakers I would write of love; for economists I would write of institutions. Same thing. "Institutional economics" at least holds a legitimate place in the past of my profession, even though it isn't highly esteemed today. I would write that economic development depends on the institutions we form. An "institution," as opposed to an "organization," need not be formal; it is an accustomed mode of behavior, such as "the institution of marriage" or "education as an institution."

I had not gotten far into my theory when I began to realize the subject was much too broad. To be credible, I had to select one institution and trace it over history. But which one? The legal system? Business corporations? The monetary system? Parliamentary democracy?

The choice was easy: it would be land tenure. How people behave with respect to land; who has the right to use it, for what; who has obligations to pay land taxes, to let others use land or share the product seemed to me at the heart of both economics and personal relations in agrarian societies. Until the industrial revolution, most societies were agrarian. Food was the most important product. For many third-world countries, this is so today.

How did the various rights and obligations over land come into being? How have they changed over the centuries? Were these changes any different in rich countries from changes in poor countries? Did land monopolists coerce peasants? Do they still? If in some places they have ceased to do so, why? So I put aside *The Horizon Society* and started on *The Story of Land: A World History of Land Tenure and Agrarian Reform*. In 1981-82, my university granted me a year's leave of absence with full pay to work on it; the Lincoln Institute of Land Policy made me a grant to cover research assistance; and Harvard University appointed me a Visiting Scholar to consult its faculty and use its libraries.

In that study, I decided that, historically, there are two kinds of land reforms, by which rights are transferred from rich to poor: reforms "by grace," offered by governments who advocate the poor, and reforms "by leverage," negotiated by the poor from their own strength.

Reforms by grace are known in antiquity: in Greece, Egypt, Rome, China, all through the Middle Ages, and right down to the present day. Reforms by leverage are rarer, and - I discovered - occurred primarily in northwest Europe and Japan, beginning about 900 A.D. It seemed to me that 900

A.D. was also about the time that northwest Europe and Japan began to split off from the rest of the world in those characteristics that later led to advanced economic development. Was there some relationship between land reform and economic development?

Another finding: all the reforms by grace were ultimately reversed, but many of the reforms by leverage lasted. Why? Because reforms by grace required powerful governments to grant them, and what government gave it could also take away; and ultimately it or its powerful successor would do so. But reforms by leverage - the principal way that feudalism was dismantled in Europe and Japan - required power by the peasantry, which the lords could not reverse, much though they tried.

But *The Story of Land* did not finish easily. The final chapter was to have covered land reforms of the Third World today. Would the twentieth century be something different, or would the same score on reforms by grace and reforms by leverage be chalked up? Since virtually all post-World-War-II land reforms are by grace, are they all doomed to failure?

There were too many for a single chapter. So, wondering if I would *ever* get any book finished, once again I set aside the one I was working on and turned to another. This time, however, I solicited a co-author - Richard Stock - to do most of the research. We found that usually but not always, the twentieth century is not different from history. But it will take me until Part Two before I say why, and why I think much sympathy for present-day land reforms is misguided.

The Peasant Betrayed: Agriculture and Land Reform in the Third World is now completed. I have also wound up *The Story of Land*, and five years after the project began, both books have gone to press. As I turn once more to *The Horizon Society*, it is time to report to the Society of Friends, so - in between writing chapters on that book - I slip in

Facing Social Revolution: The Personal Journey of a Quaker Economist.

Chapter 3

Affirmation

After our return from Kenya - with the weight of my feelings toward the Third World still upon me - Robin (my wife) and I attended a Quaker gathering in a campground in the Rockies. Kenya was all the more in our minds because we had brought our safari tent with its huge awning, a style that had once protected British colonialist-hunters from the sun as their African servants brought them tea. Now there were no British colonialists, no servants bringing tea, no sun, just twenty Quakers huddled under the canvas to protect us from a cold Wyoming downpour.

As Quakers do, we shared our inmost thoughts. They were of two types. One was affirmation for the self. Friends seemed to need to say out loud that we respect ourselves. "If I don't love myself, how can I love others?" I recalled one Friend who, on another occasion, had declared, "If I were God, making me over again, I would make me just as I am now."

The other thought was of great disappointment for our country. Our government was throwing its weight around the world, coercing and exploiting others rather than persuading and helping them. The administration spoke falsehoods, betraying our people and those outside. We were rich at the expense of the world's poor, these Friends were saying.

Quite apart from whether these affirmations were true or not, I was struck by the emotional contrast. We were proud of ourselves, yet ashamed of our society. The pride in ourselves seemed to arise not from a belief that we were superior - Friends were not bragging - but from a need of self-respect for its own sake. "I am a child of God," I kept hearing, "I have an inner light." But somehow we felt we did not *need* a respect for our society. I even wondered if, emotionally, we needed to disrespect it. Would, perhaps, our social mission be all the stronger if the society we were to correct were all the poorer?

We took down the safari tent, packed our car, and returned to Colorado. For the moment, my mind had left the Third World. I was thinking of home, Friends, and America.

We are right in our need for self-respect and self-love. To improve ourselves we must draw on our strengths. But first we must recognize them. Imagine a total derelict, good for nothing. He or she is lying in the gutter, filthy, soaked in drink and drugs, has not done honest labor in years, hates everyone; well, you name whatever else you can think of. Suppose you were assigned to rehabilitate that person. You would not say to him or her: "Why, you dirty no-good! Look at your clothes! Why don't you take a bath? Don't you know that drink and drugs harm your body?" Why wouldn't you say these things? Because they are unkind, and they wouldn't work. With your belief in the inner light, you would find something good to support.

Why do we not do the same for our society? One reason is that we are so busy fighting the MX missile, reducing the military budget, rescuing the safety-net for the poor, that we do not think of the good. As we shore up our defenses against the bad, evil commands our mind. One Friend, who had recently visited another country, told me she was taken aback when a resident of that country had said to her: "Friend, why do you hate your country so?" She resolved to think of four good things associated with the United States, and by morning - she confided - she had thought of three.

Berger (1986) wrote that "an enduring human community requires a belief in its essential rightness." Should we not find the good in our history and our present, and seek to build on that?

Chapter 4

From Socialism at Andover to the Land Grabbers of Cali

In high school in Andover, Massachusetts, I was a socialist. When I put socialist literature on the school bulletin board, the headmaster called me in to ask if I was a communist. "No, just a socialist," I said. "I suppose that's all right," he said.

In college, I marched down Boylston Street, Boston, in a parade, singing, "Solidarity forever, for the union makes us strong." Between college and graduate school I worked in New York. There I joined the Young Friends and black friends, including Bayard Rustin, in their sit-ins to test whether restaurants would serve blacks. We found that Horn and Hardart did serve blacks and we could not afford the restaurants that might not.

I became a pacifist and joined Fifteenth Street Meeting. I chuckled over the old joke, "How do you get to Washington?" "Go to Harvard and turn left." I did both and landed in Washington.

There I met Tom Carroll of the Inter-American Development Bank, an ardent supporter of land reform and a kind, sensitive person who influenced me much. He came as invited lecturer to my classes at the School of Advanced International Studies, Johns Hopkins, and I reciprocated by appearing in his seminars at the Bank. I came to support strongly government expropriation of land to redistribute to tenant farmers. I sympathized with Fidel Castro, and I went to the Swiss Embassy, which was handling Cuban affairs, to translate so Ed Snyder of the Friends Committee on National Legislation could get a visa for Cuba.

I knew of the maldistribution of income and power within the Third World, but I rationalized it by thinking, "we must help governments of the Third World, and when they are stronger, they will resolve the distribution problems in their own way."

Long before going to Kenya, however, I sensed a few doubts. In Washington, I knew people who knew the President, and it was a heady feeling to listen to first-hand stories. I also had professional assignments in all the Latin American countries except Cuba; I have met presidents or ex-Presidents of Bolivia, Colombia, Peru, Costa Rica, and Mexico, and ministers of finance and governors of central banks in many countries. It gave a false sense of importance to be hobnobbing in such high circles, and I could see that the Latin American *funcionarios* who likewise hobnobbed were possessed by a sense of their own worth. I worried that the "headiness" was inconsistent with my Quakerism and that the *funcionarios* and I felt arrogantly certain of what to do for the poor. None of us ever consulted the poor about what they might think or want.

In 1960, I taught for one semester in the University of San Andrés, Bolivia. My students all defined themselves as Marxists. For the first time, I began to be aware of the belief, which I later found to be widely held, that the sole reason for Latin American underdevelopment lay in the rapaciousness of the United States. Only a year earlier, I might have felt totally on their side. But now I saw them as I had seen myself and the Latin American *funcionarios*: feeling all-wise, they knew what to do for the poor; all they needed was power. In fact, like me they had neither been poor nor known any poor. We talked about that, too. Up until then, I had been a strong critic of American foreign policy, but when I found American policy being treated as the *sole* agent of poverty, I began to relent. For the first time, I was cast in the role of *defending* my country, for the few good things that I thought it might have done.

It was all in good spirits. The students told me that they would have fought with Fidel Castro and Che Guevara if they could have, and they would be revolutionaries in Bolivia if the occasion should arise. But we laughed together, feasted together, and met each other with *abrazos*. When classes were suspended because I had hepatitis, these goodhearted students came in groups to see me at my bedside, and when I left their country finally, they had a big party for me. I went home and wrote my first book on economic development: *Latin America: Today's Economic and Social Revolution* (McGraw-Hill, 1964), which told (as I explained in the preface) what Bolivian students "said to me and what I said to them." I might have added, "also what I would have said if I had thought of it at the time."

In 1964, while teaching at the University of Pittsburgh, I went to Colombia to lecture in favor of land reform. After my talk, the landlords' association protested vehemently to the U.S. Ambassador against the American "communist professor" coming to their country. I have a scrapbook full of editorials condemning me vituperatively in newspapers of all major Colombian cities. Officials of a Pittsburgh-based multinational corporation heard about me and complained to the University, obliquely threatening to withdraw its financial support. But Chancellor Litchfield explained academic freedom to them and said the University did not restrain its professors from saying what they believed.

One day, in Cali, Colombia, in 1963, I stumbled upon a land invasion. Sixteen thousand homeless people had seized a piece of land whose ownership had been in dispute between two prominent families ever since independence (1819). They had set up temporary symbols of houses (*chocitas*) which they would occupy until given the right to buy. I met the leaders of the invasion and spent two days walking from *chocita* to *chocita* talking to the invaders. I was warmed by their aspirations, their willingness to pay even though they could hardly pay the market price, their desire that nothing be given to them without work, their feeling of confident insistence but little antagonism toward a repressive government.

As I was about to leave, the assistant leader of the invasion asked me to come back the next day at three o'clock. "Why?" I asked. "Because the army will be here to rout us, and I want you to see it." My flight to Bogotá would leave at three, and officials of the central bank would be at the airport to meet me. But I had to disappoint them. I was back at the invasion at three, with American friends Luigi and Sylvia, who had a Volkswagen.

An hour before the army came, the invasion leader waved the Colombian flag, which was the signal for all to gather. "The army is coming," he called. "Remember the principles: NO VIOLENCE. When the army asks you to leave, leave your *chocita*. But do not go away. Stand off the field but beside it, and stay until the army goes. We can wait longer than they will." I marveled that the leaders, a handful of men and women in their twenties, would urge a crowd of 16,000 homeless people to nonviolence.

Yet what they asked for happened. I saw the army come, truckload after truckload, with bayonets drawn. They moved to the center of the field, then fanned out. The invaders sat by their *chocitas*, singing the national anthem to display their loyalty, until the soldiers came, and when told to leave, they left. The most impressive sight I have ever seen in my life was 16,000 homeless Colombians, standing several deep in a line a quarter of a mile long, facing a deployment of soldiers who surrounded the field as their *chocitas* were burned.

We did not stay to see the outcome. The assistant leader came to Luigi, half covering his face with a newspaper. "They have just arrested (the leader)," he said, "and they are looking for me. Will you drive me into town?" Knowing what would happen if we were caught, Luigi and Sylvia nevertheless did not hesitate. The assistant leader squeezed himself between the front and back seats of the Volkswagen; we covered him with a blanket, then pushed the front seats back as far as they would go. Luigi and Sylvia sat in front and I in back, my feet on top of the blanket. Hearts in mouth, we drove through the military lines, but no one stopped us.

Later I learned that the line of people did outstay the soldiers and did return to the field. After several more routings, they made their peace with the city. They did not own the land, but they stayed on it and built their houses. One cheer for nonviolence.

For the first time, I began to see a new dimension to social change. Would it come about violently as champions conquer oppressors? Or from the plans I was helping to draw, and the decisions of the *funcionarios*? Or would it come from the gathering force of millions of nonviolent actions such as that one in Cali? My new mind set, which would mature in the office of the Minister of Finance in Kenya twelve years later, was already on its course.*

---

*I wrote an article about the land invasion, published in *The Reporter* (January 1964) under the title "The Land Grabbers of Cali."

Chapter 5

From the Farms and Slums of Latin America to the Radical Students of Mexico

After the land invasion of Cali, I consciously sought out the poor.

Over the next ten years, I wandered through the slums of every Latin American capital that had slums, chatting with the occupants, in Spanish in most countries, in French in Haiti, and in sign language intermixed with some Spanish words in Brazil. I asked where they came from, what they did, how much they earned, and what were their hopes. Most had migrated in from the country; many were employed at pittance wages and some were unemployed.

I trudged through farms in the backlands of Panama, Mexico, Bolivia, and Argentina. I visited land-reform cooperatives in Chile, both before and during the Allende presidency, in which I spoke with farmers about their vision of the future. Later I did the same in the slums of African countries.

I visited farms in the bush in Liberia, Nigeria, and Kenya; I went to a hunger camp by Lake Turkana in Kenya, and still later I wandered through farms in the Philippines, talking to tenant farmers and landless workers, and attending village meetings. Although the farmers and workers sympathized with populist governments such as Perón in Argentina, in all these years not one mentioned "revolution".

But I heard "revolution" from my students in Bolivia in 1960, and I was to hear it again in Mexico in 1964. While working in Mexico City that year, I began my seminars with left-wing students from the National University. They were not the *most* left-wing, who would not speak to an American. A group had actually gone to the American Embassy to ask if there were any way to go to the United States to see whether the charges of imperialism were true. The Embassy officials phoned the Mexico office of the Experiment in International Living, a student exchange organization, and the Experiment office phoned me. I was enthusiastic, but - recalling my classes in Bolivia - I suggested a series of seminars before they went. The Embassy allocated the funds, entrusted the travel to the Experiment, and I conducted the seminars as a volunteer for the Experiment.

The students replicated the Bolivians of four years earlier almost completely. They distrusted the United States, would have fought for Fidel Castro and Che Guevara if they could have, and believed the reason for Latin American underdevelopment lay in the rapaciousness of the United States. Once again I found myself saying, "maybe my country isn't as bad as you think." Still, they opened their hearts to me.

They journeyed to the United States, and upon their return, I asked them if their views had changed. No, they felt as before, but they did have a few questions. "In Philadelphia, we asked to see where the black people lived. We expected something like the slums of Mexico City," they said. "At first we thought our hosts were deceiving us, when we saw TV antennae, and cars parked in front of the houses. We would not have believed it if we hadn't seen black people walking out of the cars and into the houses." I wrote an article about that for the *Friends Journal* ("They Saw and Were Broadened," June 15, 1966).

The seminars and visits continued annually for nine years, even after I had gone home from Mexico. They took place at Johns Hopkins and the University of Colorado, depending on where I was teaching, and they included my American students.

For several years, each time I went to Mexico, the Experiment in International Living would arrange a party with the seminar alumni. Most have jobs with government or industry; they wear neckties and dresses; they object to American policy, but they are not revolutionaries.

Chapter 6

My Work Suppressed

What I am about to tell you, I have never told before, completely. I have always held back the most sensitive part. But the events are now twenty years old. Since then, they have been spread across the newspapers and told to Congress; Senator Fulbright is retired, and others involved have done the same or moved on. It can do no harm to tell the whole story now. Even so, I will change the names.

During my first year at the University of Colorado (1966), I received a phone call from Osvaldo, who had been a student at the International Monetary Fund in the 1950s, when I was teaching in its training program. He was now director of training at the Inter-American Development Bank. "If you could come and write our training materials for loan evaluation," he said, "that would be *fantástico*."

"But I don't know how the Bank evaluates its loans," I protested. "Come and learn," he rejoined. "Spend a year at the Bank, study our procedures, and then write."

When the matter had been settled, I received a call from Joseph, a former student of mine at Johns Hopkins, who was then Assistant to the Vice President of the Bank. "While you are studying the evaluation procedures, we'd like to have your comments on how effective they are," he said. "Fair enough," I told him.

The President of the Bank sent out a circular to all staff that I had top clearance and should be shown all records; all questions should be answered freely. Two professional assistants and a secretary were assigned to me. I would select my own sample of loans; I would speak to all who had participated in their evaluation, and I would go to Latin America to interview borrowers.

I had not been long on the job before I sniffed some disagreements among the staff. As I put questions to the department heads, they in turn raised questions that made me suspect that some - far from all - were dissatisfied with the Bank's procedures. I talked this over with Joseph and with the Vice-President and came out with my feelings strengthened. I sensed that the Vice-President, a North American, was at loggerheads with the President, a Latin American, and that he had wanted an outside evaluator to strengthen his position. But of course he never said so. It was only my guess.

As I examined the loan papers, I could see the problem. Being a political actor, the Bank was "required" to make loans throughout Latin America. It could not easily snub any country. But not every government was equally capable in preparing applications, and some projects were covertly political. Procedures that are *sine qua non* in any commercial bank were simply omitted.

As I plodded through the loans, I wondered to what extent I should discuss my findings with the staff. I did not want to spread the word that I was there to have heads lopped off, but I did need feedback. So I selected several department heads to whom I would confide individual items. Only a few would see the entire draft report. I found, however, that these discussions created an aura of uncertainty, and there was much rumor about what the "Powelson report" would say and whom it might threaten.

After a year and a quarter, I had finished. "The report itself will be your training document," I told Osvaldo, who was already privy to its main ideas. Since it criticized Bank procedures, I wanted to be sure the report contained no errors. So before going to the President, I talked it over with Joseph, with various department heads and other officials, and with the Vice-President.

With one week left in my assignment, I received a call from Wilbert, one of these officials. "You understand that your report is dynamite," he said. "The President will never allow it to be released."

"That will be up to him," I replied. "Well," Wilbert said, "I'm going to take it to Senator Fulbright, whether you agree or not. Do you want to come along?"

It was not an easy choice. My first voice told me, "No, No, you would violate a confidence." My second voice rejoined, "But you have worked hard for over a year; all will be wasted if the report is suppressed. Powerful people have no right to hold back information paid for by the public and in the public's interest to know. That's what 'leaking' is for."

I wavered, I rationalized, and what I did next I have not told anyone, even my beloved wife, until now. I went along with Wilbert, telling myself that he, not I, was leaking the report. He handed over the report. I would not lay hands on it. We had a short discussion with the Senator's legislative assistants, and we returned to the Bank.

On my last day in the Bank, I asked for an appointment with the President.

He smiled as I came into his office and asked whether I was pleased with my training materials. After assuring him that I was, I handed him the report. "Sr. Presidente," I said, "Aquí tiene mi informe."

"Qué?" he asked, perplexed, "qué informe?" (What? What report?)

"El informe sobre el estudio que Usted me encargó." (The report on the study that you assigned to me).

He recovered quickly. "Gracias," he said. We shook hands; I left his office, and the next day I returned to the University of Colorado.

I soon learned, second hand, that the President was extremely angry with me, and he had indeed suppressed the report. All existing copies were to be put into the safe, never to be released. The rumor mill was churning faster than ever.

Shortly afterwards, Wilbert called me on the phone. "Do I have your permission to take the report to the *Washington Post* and *Barron's Financial Weekly*?" By then I was worried. I had intended only to jolt the Bank into improving its methods, not to create a scandal that might jeopardize its financing by Congress. This time I said "No," but I knew he would do it anyway.

The next events happened fast. A phone call from the *Washington Post*. They would do a feature article on the Bank, and did I have anything to say? Only that I had made some criticisms of policy that I hoped the Bank would correct, but that they did not represent lack of confidence in it as an institution. "We have already seen what you wrote," the reporter said. There followed a full-page article in the *Post* (12-14-69). Although the "Powelson report" was brought up only in the middle, I understand the article would not have been written but for it. Jack Anderson devoted one column (2-3-70) to a despicable, personal attack on the Bank President, using my report as its source. I felt devastated. *Barron's Financial Weekly* published a full-front-page "exposé" (10-26-70), which spilled over inside, sharply condemning the Bank and suggesting that Congress should think twice about the next funding bill. Then came the call from Senator Proxmire's office.

The omnibus funding bill was coming up for review, which would finance not only the Inter-American Bank but the World Bank and the International Monetary Fund as well. Distraught that I might have been agent provocateur for the Right, I went to the legal counsel of the Bank. Soothingly, he assured me that my report was far from being the sole, or even the major, issue. I didn't know whether to be reassured or deflated. He urged me to speak frankly before the Senate committee, but he would offer no advice, for fear it would be construed as Bank interference.

Senator Proxmire was friendly, as I sat in the witness box facing him and his committee. "How can you expect an international lending agency to improve itself," I asked, "if whenever it asks for criticism it jeopardizes its funding?" The Senator saw the point.

When the heat of the battle had passed, I learned that - with one minor exception - the Bank had implemented all my proposals within the next year. I was not invited back to examine whether this was so. But I understand that the Senate Finance Committee had maintained the pressure until it was satisfied.

My emotions ranged from deep embarrassment at having gone to Senator Fulbright to elation that my work had not been in vain. When later I would contrast this experience with the meeting in the office of the Minister of Finance in Kenya, where vital decisions were made by a single individual and Parliament was a rubber stamp; where 'leaking' would be equated to treason and subject to imprisonment, I took one more step toward believing that our own institutions have something to say for themselves after all.

Chapter 7

The Glittering Chamber of Johannesburg

The final jolt came in South Africa. From Kenya in 1974, I was invited by the African (black) Federation of Chambers of Commerce to talk to black businesspeople in several cities. Robin also was invited.

On the way south, we visited Tanzania, Zambia, and Malawi, where I lectured in universities and government agencies and enjoyed meals with professors and government officials. In Dar es Salaam I talked at the university, where I was greeted kindly by Tanzanian students but was insulted by several Canadians who wanted only to know who had paid my way - the U.S. Information Agency had - and they would listen to me no further. In Lusaka, Zambia, I found a team of Harvard Business School professors advising government officials on negotiating strategy vis-à-vis multinational corporations.

In South Africa, our hosts were Sam Motsuenyane, President of the African Federation of Chambers of Commerce (black), and Cyril Pearce, President of the Johannesburg Chamber (white). Sam and Cyril were close friends, having traveled together to other African countries to show that a prominent black and a prominent white from South Africa could do just that. In Johannesburg, Sam was often a guest at the Pearce household.

For a week, Robin and I traveled from city to city, where I told black businesspeople how racial integration had worked in Kenya, and they told us how they planned to work for it through successful black businesses in South Africa. We met Lucy Mvubela, head of the women's garment workers union, who felt that the most important goal then was recognition for black unions, achieved later, and who opposed economic sanctions, which would jeopardize her workers' jobs.

I gave a lecture at the University of Witwatersrand, with many whites and one black student in the audience. He was allowed to study there because no black university carried his program. Robin and I talked for an hour with Gatsha Buthelezi, Chief of the Zulus, the major black politician of South Africa who has stood for *nonviolent* change and who has since been much maligned in the United States for doing so. We were impressed by Chief Gatsha's poise, his determination, and his openness.

Buthelezi also opposed sanctions, for the same reasons as Lucy Mvubela. So did most of the black businessmen, for fear their businesses would be harmed. My recollection is that Sam Motsuenyane also opposed them, but twelve years later the *New York Times* (9/28/86: p.E3) reported that he was in favor.

At a dinner in Johannesburg given for us by the U.S. Embassy, I sat next to the personnel manager of an IBM plant. He was black. He told me of IBM's policy of racial integration: that all petty Apartheid, such as separate lavatories and dining facilities, had long since been abolished; that job promotion was based on performance, not on race; and that white people sometimes worked under black managers, a rarity for South Africa. All this was long before the Sullivan Code! It was therefore with some sadness that I read twelve years later - on October 22, 1986 - that IBM was quitting South Africa because of the pressure of sanctions. I wondered what would happen to that manager and to those policies.

At the close of our visit, I was asked to be the speaker at the annual banquet of the Johannesburg (white) Chamber of Commerce. When I heard that Sam was not invited, I was myself reluctant. But Sam urged me to go, saying my voice was needed.

The banquet was held in a glittering Victorian hotel, with raised speaker's table, white linen and sparkling silverware, black waiters impeccably dressed, white guests in tuxedos and long gowns. I had to rent a black-tie outfit. I sat next to the mayor of Johannesburg and Robin next to his wife. Robin was also next to Cyril Pearce and I next to Kate, his wife. In my talk after dinner, I said nothing about the economics of South Africa. Rather, I spoke on economic development in Africa as a whole.

During the dinner, however, I felt increasingly uncomfortable and artificial. At the end of my talk, I could stand it no longer. So I told the audience of my discomfort. What I said next was reported in the *Rand Daily Mail* (5-17-74) as follows:

> Professor Powelson shocked guests of the JCC at the annual banquet in Johannesburg on Tuesday night . . . (he) told the guests that had it not been for his friendship with Mr Pearce* he would not have accepted the invitation . . .
>
> "Back in the States, I would certainly not attend a gathering where any of my fellow human beings were excluded because of their ethnic origin," he said.

There followed a hushed silence that seemed an eternity. Then one table of guests, in a far corner of the

---

*The only inaccuracy in the report of the *Daily Mail* was that I had cited my friendship with Mr. Motsuenyane as well.

room, stood up, clapped and cheered, every one of them. I later learned they were visitors from Australia.

When the meeting broke, few spoke to me. Those who did admonished me for not understanding the situation. Then the reporter from the *Rand Daily Mail* asked whether, because I was a civil servant of Kenya, my visit signified an impending rapprochement between Kenya and South Africa. I said the idea had never occurred to me, and my Minister did not even know where I was. I had simply taken leave. The reporter was incredulous at my naiveté and asked whether I did not think I would be fired on my return. "Possibly," I said. In his article on page 1 the next day, he reported that I might be sacked as a Kenyan civil servant for visiting South Africa.

Since I knew that in Kenya there were South Africa watchers, upon my return I went straight to the Resident Representative of the Ford Foundation, my employer, and the Permanent Secretary of Finance and Planning, my boss, to tell them about that article before they heard it elsewhere. Both were furious. The Permanent Secretary asked whether I didn't realize what an embarrassing situation I had created for the government.

"Already," he said, "we are criticized for refueling South African planes." These planes, with other airline insignia painted on them, would land in Nairobi, to avoid an expensive detour en route to Europe. The Permanent Secretary and the Resident Representative consulted with each other; the Resident Representative offered to send me home immediately; the Permanent Secretary replied that I would leave shortly anyway, and kicking me out now would only foster adverse publicity.

Later that month the President of the Ford Foundation, visiting Kenya, also admonished me. "If we assigned you to Egypt," he asked - this was before Camp David - "you wouldn't feel you could give a lecture in Israel, would you?"

"Why not?" I replied. "The Foundation has bought my professional expertise, not my soul."

All that foppishness, all the deceit of refueling planes while calling for sanctions; the writing of sanctimonious economic plans that would mainly strengthen the corrupt rich; the political selection of whom we will talk to and whom we may not; all the headiness of power; the scant respect for the poor nor willingness to listen to them - all that I had found disgusting, in both myself and the people with whom I worked. Yes, the high mucky-mucks of the Third World were no better and no worse than our own mucky-mucks. What to do but retreat and write?

Chapter 8

What, Me a Conservative?

As I settled in to read history, speak and teach, and to write for *Friends Bulletin*, *Friends Journal*, and Pendle Hill, I was astonished to discover I was gaining the reputation among Quakers of being a conservative. What, me? Socialist at Andover, who sang Solidarity Forever in Boston, whom the landlords in Colombia had called a communist, who had caused a multinational corporation to threaten the University of Pittsburgh? Me, now a conservative? One friend wrote me that "your articles in the *Friends Journal* enrage our local Meeting, but I guess that's not news to you, is it?" Another complained that I had never shown any sympathy for the thousands of people being killed in El Salvador. I can't quote his exact words, because I tore the letter up.

I began to take stock. I hold a central belief: in the *dispersion* of power, in the safeguards of pluralism or of numerousness of political groupings and their ability to hold each other accountable for the use of resources, financial, human, and ecological. I oppose concentrations of power, whether in multinational corporations, labor unions, or governments, be they socialist or capitalist. All of these agencies are all right in reasonable dimension; when they overpower, each becomes mainly wrong.

One friend said to me, "The difference between us is that you don't believe government can do anything right, and I believe it can." That too hurt. But he had not known third-world governments as I had, and it is, I suppose, natural to believe that other governments are like one's own. Many times I think our own is too powerful; but at least it has a built-in set of checks and balances, such as the Senate Finance Committee, which most of the Third World does not have.

Well, if I were to be a conservative, I decided I had better find out what conservatives are. I discovered they come in branches, just like liberals and radicals, and one branch I do not accept is that which favors the power of the United States and nuclear arms, and which opposes government programs for the poor. But what is there, etymologically, in the word "conservative" that gives that branch the right to apply it to themselves?

Grace Goodell, a conservative anthropologist who has influenced my thinking much, one day handed me *The Conservative Mind*, by Russell Kirk (1958). I later read in the *Wall Street Journal* that Kirk has been dubbed "Mr. Conservative" in the United States. His is a solid, mind-provoking book. Among his most insightful passages, I found this paragraph on Edmund Burke (p. 19):

> He had defended the liberties of Englishmen against their king, and the liberties of Americans against king and Parliament, and the liberties of Hindus against Europeans. He had defended those liberties not because they were innovations, discovered in the Age of Reason, but because they were ancient prerogatives, guaranteed by immemorial usage. *Burke was liberal because he was conservative* [emphasis added].

The phrase about Burke's being liberal because he was conservative kept coming back to me. But I would interpret Burke in terms of my own condition. Living in a different age, he probably would not have agreed totally with my political philosophy. But I believe that all persons are capable of influencing their own economic and social destinies, *provided* they have the opportunity themselves to shape the institutions that protect their liberties and guarantee them a reasonable share of the common weal.

These institutions are forged slowly, by negotiation more than by war, and we must not be impatient because they are not yet all in place. As they are forged, they must be conserved. I could not be a liberal without being conservative, nor a conservative without also being liberal.

PART TWO

THE JOURNEY IN HISTORY

Chapter 9

The Poor Can Empower Themselves

> Who advocates the peasant? Do Marxist revolutionary governments? Do the governments of "capitalist" countries? Do the governments of the more developed world? Does the government of the Soviet Union, or China? Do private agencies like Oxfam and the American Friends Service Committee? (*The Peasant Betrayed*, first paragraph of concluding chapter).

For over three centuries, Friends have answered the cries of the hungry, the imprisoned, the oppressed. Drought victims in Ethiopia, blacks in South Africa, refugees from Central America are modern testimony to this calling.

For the most part, our response has been direct and quiet. The cause of the suffering was not for us to fathom; the fact of it was enough. But Friends also have sought - through sit-ins, boycotts, legislation - to change the institutions that enable the oppressors to oppress. The underground railroad for escaped slaves was direct action; John Woolman's travels bespoke the quiet persuasion.

Mainly, Friends have worked through our own institutions: Quaker Peace and Service (London), American Friends Service Committee, Friends Committee on National Legislation, Friends World Committee, and the like. However, with the emergence of the Third World as independent polities, we have moved beyond our small circle. We have tried to help third-world governments in their attempts to spur economic development and to provide for their poor.

Friends have felt especially supportive of governments that have undertaken land reform, social services, and education in rural areas, and have provided credit, technical assistance, seed, and fertilizer for small farmers. I have joined Friends in these feelings.

To one like me, who has rallied emotionally and in full dedication to these third-world governments, the book I co-authored confirmed the shock and disillusionment I had already felt in working for those governments. In *The Peasant Betrayed*, Richard Stock and I tried to discover how well the governments are performing in their quests to develop economically and to help their poor. Sadly, we concluded that with a few exceptions, these governments have harmed the rural poor far more than they have helped them, and further, that it mattered not whether the government was "socialist" such as Algeria, Cuba, China, and Tanzania, or "capitalist" such as Egypt, Indonesia, Mexico, and Somalia. Each proclaimed itself for the peasant, yet each betrayed the peasant sorely.

Whether a government systematically exploits its poor or honestly tries to help them, once it arrogates to itself the role of champion it does not empower the poor but acts and decides in their stead. All too often - nay, nearly always - the champion's program for the poor is *not* what the poor would have chosen for themselves; the poor know better than the champion what will benefit them most, but their wisdom is disregarded.

Why does the champion fail to benefit the poor? Mainly because he or she depends on power. The champion has therefore created a power *position*, to be occupied by himself or herself. But some or all of four things always happen.

First, the qualities of a champion are not those of a governor. Revolutionary officers and radical intelligentsia are not well trained in politics and economics, even the students I knew in Bolivia and Mexico; and when they are, their own power overwhelms them, and they think that economic laws that constrain others do not apply to them.

Second, they themselves or their underlings become corrupted. If by utmost exception they retain their integrity, they still cannot control the society by themselves, and they must delegate power to local officials, who may be corrupt.

Third, revolutionary government officials are mortal, and their successors are not as benevolent as they themselves claim to be.

Fourth, their power position attracts or threatens others. Either the attracted or the threatened will take the power away from them if they can.

For one or all these reasons, the governments promoting "liberation," such as Algeria, Bolivia, Chile, China, Cuba, Egypt, Iran, Libya, Mexico, Soviet Union, Tanzania, and Vietnam, have failed to liberate the poor. Nicaragua is failing now; it will continue to fail whether the Contras win or lose; and so will El Salvador, no matter which side wins the war in that country.

Do you believe the title to this chapter, that the poor *can* empower themselves? I do, for I have seen it in history. But I tried other titles in earlier drafts. I started with, "Empower the Poor," but that implies that someone else would do it for them. Whoever does so would become the champion, with all the hazards of rescinding the gift just as he or she had endowed it.

Next I experimented with, "Let (or May) the poor be empowered." That one has two problems. First, "let" or "may" implies that someone grants permission, so that person would be the champion. Second, "be empowered" implies that the matter just happens, whereas in fact, I believe, the poor must empower themselves. I thought of how the French and Spanish use "que" with both subjunctive and reflexive: "Que les pauvres se rendent puissants" or "Que los pobres se hagan poderosos." ("That the poor shall empower themselves"). That sounded paternalistic, as if I were transmitting my wishes about the poor. So I settled for a simple statement that I believed the poor could do it.

When I question the benevolence of the Sandinistas in Nicaragua, I am occasionally asked, "Would you prefer Somoza?" But that is like asking, "Had you been a Russian in the 1920s, would you have preferred the Czar over the Soviets? If a Frenchman in the 1790s, Louis XVI over Robespierre? As a Mexican in the 1920s, Porfirio Díaz over Calles? In all these cases, history has passed on, and the real question is, "Are the programs of Robespierre, Stalin, Calles, and the Sandinistas the right ones, or is something better possible?"

My first voice asks me: You speak of political rights: the freedom to vote, to seek one's own job, to move where one will. But what of economic rights? Do the peasants not have the right to be fed, to be educated, to own land? Then my second voice answers: That question assumes that by taking away the peasant's political rights, the champion might offer economic rights. No, no, my second voice goes on, only the peasant is his or her own champion. Only with political rights will the peasant possess the leverage to gain economic rights. If we wish to help the poor, we must help them empower themselves, to defend themselves against their oppressors, their champions, and - yes - against us.

Why does the champion go wrong? The four ways I have just mentioned are general. How does it happen *specifically*? Let us give the champion the benefit of the doubt - a real doubt in my mind - and suppose that he or she is committed, benevolent, and generous,. does not seek power for its own sake, but truly wishes to help the poor. The revolutionary government has just confiscated land monopolized by the wealthy, the oppressors. Why does it not simply divide this land among the tenants? Here are some reasons usually given:

First, there are many landless besides the tenants. To whom would it give land? How much? Would not the new owners become the nucleus of new oppression? Is it not better to socialize the land, in "cooperatives" or in state farms? I use quotation marks because to me, cooperatives are voluntary, but state "cooperatives" are not.

Second, the farmers - so long under the heels of their landlords - do not have enough credit. If they go to ordinary banks, they will be overcharged for interest, or so it is alleged. Far better that the government should supply the credit, and it can do so more easily to "cooperatives" or nationalized farms.

Third, peasants are presumed not to know how to buy their seed and fertilizer or sell their crops without others taking advantage of them. If they buy from "capitalists" or "middlemen," will they not pay too much? If they try to sell on their own, will not "monopolists" cheat them or offer too low a price? Far better that the state - instead of the landlord or the free market - should organize production, credit, supply inputs, and buy the product, or so it is argued. Of course, for the state to perform this task well, it must usually be the sole buyer, sole seller, or sole banker. Therefore, the peasants are not allowed to do business with others.

Finally, if land were given outright to the peasants, who might not understand its full value and are probably so hungry that they want immediate cash, will they not sell it and find themselves totally dispossessed? These have been roughly the reasons advanced by all the governments I have mentioned, socialist and non-socialist alike.

Are these explanations valid? I think not - for two reasons: one, because the peasant is not as ignorant as the reasons imply; and two, because certain "unexpected" results occur frequently. Let us leave the "ignorance" of the peasant for the next chapter and turn now to the "unexpected" results.

First, *as a whole* peasants do not want to join the "cooperative" or state farm. There is a long history of peasants, all over the world, resisting "cooperatives" set up by the state, although if allowed, they will form cooperatives of their own design. Of course, many will vigorously acclaim the new government, and these will be the ones most noticed by outside supporters. But the real question is: What would *all* the peasants decide if given a real choice? In not one of the countries that we studied was such a choice given. Sometimes, as in Nicaragua, the peasant is nominally free to choose, but the penalty exacted for not joining is great, such as denial of access to credit, seed, or fertilizer on the same terms as other farmers. In short, join the "cooperative" or risk going out of business.

Second, even when the peasant is in the "cooperative" or state farm, the problems begin rather than end. Cheap credit cannot be provided to everyone; demand for it exceeds its supply. The government may print money to meet the demand, but inflation reduces its value. If the amount of credit is restricted, richer farmers or those with political clout receive most, as we found in Mexico. There much "ejidal" credit (credit for collective farms) was concentrated in one politically-favored area.

Third, the government runs into financial troubles. Perhaps it cannot collect the taxes it expected; perhaps corrupt officials pocket the proceeds; perhaps its nationalized enterprises incur losses. All these problems we found in our case studies. To recoup its losses, the government *increases* the prices of fertilizer and seed rather than decreasing them; it pays *less* for crops instead of more.

Fourth - probably the greatest problem of all - is that in the press for development, the government must serve its urban constituency. Some revolutionary governments have spoken of a "worker-peasant alliance," in which city and rural poor have jointly sought freedom from their earlier oppressors. In our studies, we found no such alliance formed naturally, only where government had required it. Instead, the interests of rural farmers and urban workers conflicted. Urban workers demand cheap food. To satisfy them, the government puts a ceiling on farm prices, setting it so low that farmers cannot meet their costs. Result: they abandon their farms and join the mass migration into cities, where they live in slums, supported by charity of relatives, until they can find jobs, if ever.

Because of this abandonment and these policies, in many countries agricultural output has fallen. *For twenty years in the 1960s and 1970s, the average annual per capita food production fell: in Algeria by 1.85%; in Botswana by 2.56%; in Egypt by 0.40%; in Somalia by 2.43%; and in Zambia by 1.21%.* In Tanzania, farm production increased by 2.31% per capita per year during the 1960s, before policies like the ones described above were initiated. Once the policies were in effect, it fell by 1.80% *per year* during the 1970s.* A drop of 1.80% per year, compounded for ten years, amounts to about 16.6% altogether.

These grim statistics must be taken against the background of outstanding success elsewhere in third-world agriculture, the output of which has grown by about 4.4% per year in recent years (NYT 9/9/86). But this growth has been confined to those countries that have largely left the

*Figures from Food and Agriculture Organization of the United Nations, *Production Yearbook*, volumes 26 (for 1961-71) and 37 (for 1972-1983). They are cited, along with data for other countries, in *The Peasant Betrayed*, page 283.

farmers alone on their *own* land, making their own decisions. Bangladesh, which ten years ago was considered a "basket case," is now feeding itself well, and India apparently has thrown off the scourge of perennial famine. But whatever goodwill is manifest by governments championing the peasant, the programs they have coerced peasants into have failed, and the people cannot be fed if the fields do not produce enough.

Economists explain the reduction in output by the loss of incentives. No reward, no production. Another possible explanation, which researchers have not adequately examined, lies in the psychology of choice, or as some psychologists say, "learned helplessness." Psychologists have found that people who make choices in their occupations are more effective than those who simply follow orders.* When the government makes the main decisions over crop, price, where to buy and sell, requiring compliance, and the farmer has little or no choice, he or she may lose heart.

The shriveled and dying drought victims of Africa are a most tragic example of misguided policies. Droughts are a perennial for Africa; they have long been serious. In the past, however, tribes have been able to cope. The chief would store food in good years, or tribes would help each other if the drought was not universal.

Now, however, the requirement to sell all crops to government has made storage impossible, and the low prices have discouraged many from farming at all. The government has squandered the crops, paying the proceeds to corrupt politicians. Some chiefs who have stored for the next famine have been accused of being "hoarders" and have had crops

---

*This idea came after conversation with Steven Maier, Professor of Psychology at the University of Colorado, one of the principal researchers on "learned helplessness."

confiscated. Some who have kept lands in honest fallow to restore fertility have lost them to a land reform in which "idle land" was seized. Thus the tribes have lost their ability to cope. Now dependent on government handouts, they find that corrupt politicians, or politicians who consider them "enemies" as in Ethiopia, deny them their subsistence.

This problem is increasingly recognized in the press. In the first chapter of *The Peasant Betrayed*, we present a collection of citations from various newspapers. Too late for inclusion in that book, here is yet another (from the *Washington Post Weekly*, 9/1/86):

> The U.N. Food and Agriculture Organization says most African countries adopted policies that gave farmers little incentive to grow more food than their own families could eat. Instead, these policies lured many farmers, the backbone of poor African economies, to cities. There, they stopped farming and started eating imported food, purchased with overvalued currency and foreign aid money. In those years, food imports rose tenfold.

Agricultural output per capita in Nicaragua fell by about one quarter during the first years of the Sandinista government. A portion of this loss was caused by the Contras' destruction of farms, but crop shortfalls both began before the Contra fighting and occurred in areas unaffected by it. When output stagnates or declines in over twenty countries, which we studied for *The Peasant Betrayed*, and when these countries have differing political orientations but similar agricultural policies, then we must call into question the wisdom of those policies, even in the one country violated by the United States.

This chapter raises two questions, as yet unanswered:

First, given that the champion fails, what then? Does the choice lie only between the champion and the earlier oppressor? How can the poor empower themselves, when the strength of the oppressor is overwhelming? Could they really do it without a champion? This question will be the topic of much of the remainder of this book.

Second, if there is to be no champion, then what is the role for Quakers? If we cannot be champions, can we at least be advocates? How? I will address that question in Chapter 20.

But another question comes before these two: How able are the poor to champion themselves?

Chapter 10

The Myth of the Ignorant Poor

When I was a child, I heard that black people were genetically inferior to whites, even less intelligent. The belief was so common that my parents felt it necessary to teach me specifically that this was not so. By the time I had reached high school in the 1930s, most of my generation no longer believed in genetic inferiority. But two decades later in Bolivia, I was surprised when a middle-class Bolivian woman of Spanish descent told me that the Indian was impassive, mute, capable of hard work, but lacked the intelligence for higher education, to conduct a business, or to hold a government job.

Since that time, I have heard the myth of the ignorant poor in many guises. Mostly in planning offices and international institutions, where good people confuse illiteracy with ignorance. I found it among radicals who wanted to "sensitize the poor to their condition." In a discussion at Harvard, my co-panelist, a Harvard professor, was explaining the rural credit institutions needed to promote economic development. "Why not leave those to the local people?" I asked. He was horrified. "You wouldn't just leave them to fend for themselves?" he asked.

To explore the myth, we start not with the poor but with the champions.

The Champions

Except in China and perhaps a few other places, throughout the Third World the champions are of a culture distinct from the poor. The economics students I hobnobbed with in Bolivia, Mexico, and other countries felt far more at home with me than they did with Indians. Mostly, they could not talk to Indians, not knowing their language, and they knew little about what Indians believed or felt. Even in China, the poor are sometimes culturally different - for example, the Uighurs, the Mongols - but not in most parts. Of course, this general proposition must be taken relatively, for in some places the differences merge into each other, as in Indian and mestizo populations, and sometimes the poor have moved culturally into upper classes. Nevertheless, I believe that for the most part the cultural distinction is true.

In many areas, the difference is ethnic. Again except for most of China, the poor often consider themselves as belonging to different "nations" or tribes from the rulers. This point applies particularly to Africa and to Latin American countries with heavy Indian populations. But it is also true in India and throughout southeast Asia. Although Tagalog is a dominant language in the Philippines, there are many others, and, as in India, English becomes the lingua franca.

Even where the difference is not ethnic, it is felt in Westernization. Schooled in European or American universities, or in their facsimiles in their own countries, the champions often identify more with values learned there than they do with those of their native lands. In Africa, they learned them also while serving in colonial governments. Is it surprising, then, that they should hold stereotypes of their poor analogous to those that we Westerners have held - at least in the past - for our own ethnic minorities?

The Myth

Every one of the following stereotypical statements I have heard many times in the Third World, and some of them I have heard in my own country. Yet I believe that not one of them is true:

(1) The poor do not save (they are too poor to save);

(2) The poor do not have credit institutions; they do not know how to borrow or lend;

(3) The poor are conservative, obstinate. They stick to old methods of farming even when new ones are available. "Just drive through Mexico, and look at all the peasants ploughing with oxen;"

(4) If the poor were given land of their own, they would sell it for a mess of pottage or a drink at the corner bar;

(5) The poor do not conserve. If they owned their own land, they would cut down the trees for firewood and erode the soil;

(6) With such little experience the poor do not know how to enter the market place. They do not know the value of what they sell, so they will let it go cheaply, and they will pay too much for what they buy;

(7) The poor are passive and fatalist. They believe they are poor by the grace of God, and there is nothing they can do about it. If there is to be a revolution, therefore, the poor must be sensitized to their plight.

Just as in our own culture, where myths about people of other ethnic origins have served the purpose of the dominant society, so also in the Third World do myths about the poor serve the purpose of both the oppressors and the champions. If the myths were not true, why would the poor need champions? But, if the poor are so capable, what is left for Quakers to do? I believe we do have a role, and in fact we have been fulfilling it considerably. I will share more thoughts on that later.

At a recent national gathering of 1600+ Friends, a plenary session was devoted to the play, *A Peasant of El Salvador*. It has been widely shown elsewhere as well. Juan, the peasant, was played in stereotype. He was good, gentle, and uncomplaining. When his children "disappeared," he went to church and lit a candle. When he sold flowers to the rich, he did not know how much to ask for them, and they laughed at him for charging so little. When his farm was taken; when he was brutally treated as a plantation worker, he accepted all passively. Finally, the champion entered and sensitized Juan politically.

Over the past twenty years, peasants have been widely studied by a number of anthropologists and economists, and virtually all such studies show them as shrewd evaluators, quick to perceive changes in their environment. They know what their land and their products are worth and will not easily be duped. If the Mexican farmer ploughs with oxen, either oxen do the job at lower cost than motor power, given availability, repair facilities, and the like, or the farmer does not have enough money for motor power. If motor power is more profitable and the farmer does not have the money, the reason is that Mexican credit facilities are artificially closed to him, and peasant credit is not sufficient. But the reason is *not* that the peasant does not know about motor power or that he obstinately sticks to old ways.

Lele (1972) cites fifteen studies showing the capabilities of peasants. After living in peasant communities in the Philippines and Iran, Goodell (1983, 1986) concludes that villagers have their own credit mechanisms, their own markets, their own sources of fertilizer and seeds, and know more about farming than the government officials sometimes sent to advise or coerce them. In a book on agricultural economics in the Third World, Reynolds (1975:5) refers to the peasant as "a shrewd fellow who has learned through experience to allocate efficiently and who is responsive to economic incentives within his perceived opportunity set."

Some point to peasants who have cut down all the trees around them, so the soil erodes. "They don't think of their grandchildren," these critics say. But wait! Usually these trees are on common land or government land. To the individual peasant, the choice is not firewood or a tree for one's grandchild. It is one's own firewood or someone else will get it first. The grandchild won't have it in any event. If, however, the tree were on the peasant's own farm, I suspect the care would be different.

But if peasants are indeed shrewd, why do they need to be "sensitized?" Why do they need champions? Let us turn to history to see whether peasants have in the past bettered themselves without champions. If so, where?

Chapter 11

Japan, Ourselves, and the Rest of the World

Queries on Land

In much of the Third World, the powerful have become wealthy by seizing land and its product, crushing the peasants down to subsistence living. This injustice lies behind the revolutions in El Salvador and Nicaragua. In South Africa, 87% of the land is occupied by 17% of the people, who enshrine their rights in Apartheid. Is there a remedy to injustice on the land? By violence? By nonviolence? Sooner by violence than by nonviolence? Or still otherwise? What has happened in history?

More generally, does economic development in the West and Japan have anything to tell the Third World? Some say, "Economic development is economic development, just as steel is steel. You make it the same way, no matter where." Others say, "Why should the Third World follow the West or Japan? Might it not develop in its own way?"

My position is in-between, but I like the steel analogy. Steel is not the same everywhere, but there are certain core ingredients: iron, other minerals, energy. You can mix them differently, use different kinds of energy; you can make different kinds of steel. So also the ways of economic development are many. But there are common ingredients. We must study history to know what is common and what is unique. We must study history to discover whether social justice leads to peace or peace to social justice, or whether war leads to either or neither. The Third World does not need to follow the West and Japan exactly, but the West and Japan are not irrelevant.

Land Reforms by Leverage

About the tenth century - when the world was still feudal or tribal - the landholding patterns of Japan and northwest Europe (northern France, western Germany, the low countries, and England) began to diverge from those of southern and eastern Europe, China, South Asia, and Middle East. Why, we do not know. The northwest European pattern reached its distinctiveness about the twelfth century, the Japanese not until the seventeenth. The greater mystery is why northwest Europe and Japan were so similar, since they did not communicate with each other that we know of, until late in the sixteenth century. Feudalism in Japan and northwest Europe turned contractual, while that of the rest of the world remained coercive.

The difference appears only in hindsight, nor is it finely drawn even then. In northwest Europe and Japan, peasants and feudal lords hammered out their relationships by bargain. In the rest of the world, servitude was totally imposed by lords upon peasants.*

At first we must not see too much in this difference, for the peasants of Europe were so socially and politically inferior to their lords that they could not make favorable bargains. In *The Story of Land*, I refer to "unequal contract," though that terminology is not original with me.

*Eastern and southern Europe, with hybrid systems, were exceptions to this generality until they restored coercive feudalism about the sixteenth century. Their situations are complex, and I do not take them up here.

What kind of bargain? In Europe, the peasants agreed to supply the lords with specified labor, so many days a week, and foodstuffs. In return, they received the use of land, over which the lords had superior rights, to grow their own crops. The lords would manage the peasants' defense, a not negligible consideration where unseen armies would strike at any time. The lords would supply the peasants with grist mills and allow them to gather wood on properties held in common. The peasants had to buy their beer from the lords. The lords had to approve peasant marriages, for which the peasants would pay a fee in kind. Peasants contracted services to their lords, and lords agreed not to abandon the peasants. And so on and on. In Japan, the story was similar with different timing.

In the rest of the world, by contrast, this contractual pattern did not evolve. That world was one of conquest, in which victors, such as Mongols, Turks, or Muslims in holy war, seized the land and virtually enslaved the peasants upon it if they did not kill them. Often they would appoint military governors whose duty was to turn over a certain amount of taxes to the emperor or sultan; how these taxes were collected was up to them. Unlike western Europe, they had right of life or death over their subjects. They did in Japan, too, until that was bargained away.

In the centuries that followed, bargaining grew and expanded in northwest Europe and Japan, but coercion remained steadfast in the rest of the world. Again, we know *what* happened but not *why*. However, if we are to draw insights on how Western/Japanese experience might help understand the Third World today, we have to make some conjecture on *why*. I will do so unabashedly, but I must distinguish between observation and interpretation.

Observation. From about the tenth century on, European peasants formed village organizations, which both conducted village business - trade, justice, settled conflicts - and negotiated with the lords over land rights. Japanese villagers also did this, but their organizations were more military. In what is now the Third World, village organizations also emerged; they were well-developed in India, for example, even before Europe/Japan. But they conducted local business only, rarely if ever bargaining with their overlords for land rights.

Observation. Peasants in Europe and Japan had a more diversified set of overlords than did those in the rest of the world. They faced noblemen of different ranks - Church officials, princes, and later town patricians. In Germany, "ministeriales," representatives of the princes, developed overlord powers of their own. Moreover, many of these overlords were in conflict with one another. In Japan, land rights on great estates (*sho-en*) were contested among nobles, managers, agents of the emperor, agents of the shogun, and so on. In what is now the Third World, by contrast, any one group of peasants was generally subject to a single overlord, such as the Turkish sipahi or janissary, the Mughal zamindar, or the Chinese emperor.

Interpretation. In these conflicts, overlords often depended on peasants. By shifting their support among overlords in Europe and Japan, peasants could bargain for better conditions. In principle, no peasant could bypass an overlord, such as a noble, appealing to a superior one, such as a prince or king. In practice, peasants sometimes did this, playing off one overlord against another.

Interpretation for Third World today. Conflicts among overlords abound in the Third World. If small farmers were better organized than they are, they might gain political advantage by shifting their weight among overlords. What power do peasants have? They produce food, without which the overlords cannot live.

Observation. As towns and commerce grew in Europe in the eleventh through thirteenth centuries, and in Japan in the seventeenth and eighteenth, village organizations enhanced their bargaining power. At first town patricians and landowners were the same people; later they began to be different; their interests diverged; and the peasants could choose sides and make their bargains. The biggest problem in towns was to assure a steady food supply at reasonable price. Landowners by contrast wanted a high price for food. Peasants now had choices. They could produce food or find jobs in town.

Observation. Simultaneous to the above, European peasants enhanced their rights in two other ways. In towns, they gained juridical freedom (were no longer serfs). On landed estates, they might select their crops, buy and sell where they wished, pay rent in money instead of in services and crops. Legally, the land still belonged to the lords, but more and more peasants *behaved* as if it were theirs.

Instead of redefining the rights of serfs, usually peasants got court orders that they were freemen and not serfs. Finally, the term "serf," like "slave" before it, went out of usage. As kings consolidated their governments vis-à-vis nobles, the ultimate right over land ("sovereignty") went to the king. So the money paid by peasants became "taxes" instead of "rent."

When laws were finally passed to abolish the legal distinction between serf land and free land, in France at the time of the Revolution, in England not until 1923, in Scotland not yet, the distinction in practice had long worn away. Land reform had occurred; the peasants owned their land. That the Duke of Bedford must cater to tourists today to maintain his great estate reflects the erosion of power of the landed aristocracy. A similar process, differing in its details, happened in Japan, mainly in the eighteenth and nineteenth centuries.

Interpretation. The peasants gained their land rights for several reasons. First, they held some power, to produce food, and the bargaining institutions were in place. Second, a free, landowning peasantry served not only the interests of the peasants themselves but also of growing business, which wanted more food for urban workers and considered feudal agriculture inefficient. Third, some farmers preferred to move to cities, where they were needed. Putting the most efficient farmers on the proper farms, and moving others into town, required that land be freely bought and sold; hence it had to be released from feudal restrictions.

Interpretation for the Third World today. Feudalism is anachronistic in the Third World today just as it was in Europe and Japan a few centuries ago. Growth of cities requires more food, and feudal farms do not produce it efficiently. These are the conditions conducive to land reform.

A word of caution. I have greatly simplified, in order to bare the essentials. The processes in Europe and Japan were not easy, not always peaceful. Peasant revolts abounded, landowners fought back, history zigzagged. But the peasant revolts were usually lost; reforms were initiated reluctantly by the very ones who had opposed them at first; the fighting of landlords dimmed over time; and history increasingly zigged more than it zagged.

Land reforms by grace

While people in northwest Europe and Japan were bargaining for their land reforms, those in the rest of the world received them by grace. In the third century B.C., kings Agis and Cleomenes of Sparta confiscated land from powerful owners, their political enemies, and distributed it to all Spartiates capable of bearing arms. Although they professed love for the poor, they were more concerned in strengthening the army; soldiers would support them in exchange for land. Once they passed on, the land reform was reversed.

In 133 B.C., the Gracchus brothers (Tiberius and Gaius) of Rome confiscated lands from large owners and divided them among landless Roman citizens. They, too, professed love for the peasants, but historians see other motives: to weaken their political enemies; to strengthen the Roman army, which could be composed only of landholders; to reduce dependency on wheat from Sicily and Africa, where deliveries had been endangered by slave revolts; and to promote widespread ownership in Rome, to decrease the danger of slave revolts there. Their reforms lasted for roughly the next century, but they were lost as landholdings became more concentrated under the Empire.

At the beginning of the first century A.D., lands owned by the Chinese nobility were not taxed, but those of the peasants were. To escape taxation, therefore, peasants had "commended" their lands and themselves to nobles. As serfs, they were better off than as taxpayers. In 9 A.D., concerned for the dwindling imperial treasury, Emperor Wang Mang confiscated land from the large owners, mainly his political enemies, and awarded it to peasants, who were promptly taxed. He too professed love for the peasantry. But corruption and peasant uprisings caused new drains on his treasury; the bureaucracy rebelled, and the reforms were reversed within three years. Wang Mang himself was overthrown twelve years later.

In the sixth and seventh centuries A.D., Chinese emperors of the Sui and T'ang dynasties confiscated lands from large holders, and - once again professing love for the peasantry - divided them equally (with some exceptions) among all male farmers of working age. These holders would keep the land until they retired, then return it to the state for redistribution. Silkworm land, by exception, could be inherited, so that farmers would be encouraged to plant mulberry bushes.

But the reform fell apart as emperors began awarding large estates to their families and political allies, exempt from taxes. Commendation returned, and within two centuries land engrossments had restored China to its large holdings and peasant serfs. Japan copied China in the Taika reforms of 645-652 - before that country had become more similar to Europe - with the same results. Similar land reforms occurred at the beginning of every Chinese dynasty thereafter except the foreign ones (Mongol and Manchu), and every one of them was reversed before the dynasty had ended.

After I had returned from Kenya and was reading histories of China, my attention was caught by the Sung Emperor's counselor, Wang An-shih, who in 1069 instituted a set of reforms for China remarkably similar to those of the Kenya five-year plan: credit for small farmers, labor surveys, fiscal planning, state trading, price stabilization, education, and improved civil service. Many of the reforms strengthened state power, just as the Kenya plan did nine centuries later. But Wang lost his job in 1074 because of political opposition, and, when the Emperor died in 1089, only those few reforms that pleased the new Emperor remained.

At the end of the twelfth century, Ghazan Khan, the Mongol ruler of Iran, became alarmed at the deterioration of the countryside. Peasants were dying wholesale; entire villages were being abandoned; crops were not being planted. One tax collector had been advised to "treat the peasants kindly and to cause them to cultivate the land." Ghazan ordered all lands to be registered, land claims to be limited to thirty years and then redistributed; taxes to be reduced to within payable amounts; and abandoned lands to be parceled out among the soldiers, who were charged with growing crops. But he was doing this to consolidate his own power, not that of the peasantry. The conclusion of historian Ann Lambton (1953) is that old habits returned the instant Ghazan's control was relaxed.

Other examples abound, but these are enough. They have in common that authoritarian land reform, granted "graciously" by a monarch "out of love for his poor," is really an instrument to consolidate his own power.

Enter the twentieth century. The first major land reform is that of the Soviet Union. As the revolutions of 1917 struck, Russian landholdings were basically of three types: those of the Crown and the nobility; those of the *mir*, communes managed by peasants but with restrictions from the state; and private peasant holdings that had been freed from the *mir* in land reforms of the past eleven years (Stolypin reforms). Immediately, lands of the Crown and nobility were put into state farms or in most cases were grabbed by peasants. By 1919, there were no more wealthy landowners; 96.8% of cultivable land was held by peasants, either through their own communes (*mir*) or privately.

For ten years (1917-1927), the Soviet government could not decide on a land policy. Although most high officials, including Lenin, Trotsky, and Stalin, wanted to collectivize, others, such as Bukharin, favored letting the peasants decide. A few peasants joined the collectives and state farms proposed by the government, but most preferred to remain with the *mir* or their private holdings. Even holdings on the *mir* functioned as private land, but they were redivided from time to time.

During this decade, the government tried to procure grain forcibly from the farmers at prices lower than cost. It changed the official prices frequently, so that farmers did not know which crops to plant. As a result, food deliveries to the city declined.

Upset by this decline, and placing the blame on greedy, private farmers, the government struck in 1927. Private farms and *mir* were invaded, farmers killed, arrested, or otherwise abused. Peasants resisted passively, the only way they could, but the army entered the farms. The *mir* was destroyed; private farms taken away. One scholar (Conquest 1986) estimates that the Soviet army killed twenty million farmers, as many as the Russian soldiers lost in World War II.

Agricultural output fell by 25% from the late 1920s to the mid-1930s. Thereafter, the experience has been mixed - in some years improved - but basically poor. Virtually all agricultural experts agree that collectivized Soviet farming has yielded far less than its potential.

To spur production, in the 1970s the Soviets began allowing farmers to sell some of their product on the free market. Like similar experiments in collectivized Algeria, Cuba, China, and Tanzania, this one has worked. Where farmers are free to grow what they like, to sell where they like at prices they themselves set, agricultural output increases along with the incomes of the poor. But in all these socialist countries except China, the "free" part of the economy is still severely curtailed. In Cuba, this freedom was withdrawn in May, 1986. And in China, the government has the power to curtail it whenever it wishes; it may do so after a political change. In none of these countries - nor in much of the Third World - are small farmers able to manage their lives freely in the same way that they came to do in Europe and Japan, through their own leverage.

A Query for Friends

Do we further the interests of the poor when we support or even give sympathetic understanding to land reforms by grace that employ coercive, sometimes violent, action against peasants to assure their participation? Do we recognize these as Moloch in a new disguise, as Jim Corbett said in his Foreword? Should not Friends, as one of the few small bodies committed to non-violence, steadfastly seek justice for peasants only by methods consistent with an ethic of love and non-violence?

From my studies of historical and present land tenure systems, I feel confident in the following observations:

. . . That no government decreeing land reform by grace has permitted the peasants to participate, through vote, counsel, or other political instrument, in deciding upon basic landholding structures, but has on the contrary usually deployed economic restrictions, physical force, or military violence to assure peasant participation;

. . . That land reforms by grace generally are reversed when the government runs into financial difficulty, or when the power it has taken unto itself rather than sharing with the peasantry is seized by someone else;

. . . That peasants, wherever they have been given an opportunity to decide the type of landholding, have preferred individual, private farms, although there are a few, idealistically motivated exceptions, such as the Israeli kibbutz and Hutterite settlements;

. . . That individual, private farms historically have provided greater incomes to the peasants and more food for the country, while collectivized agriculture, with few exceptions, is considered a failure by virtually all experts, in that it produces less food than comparable land under private ownership.

Many of us have visited Algeria, Cuba, Nicaragua, and Tanzania, returning with praise for the governments of those countries. While appreciating the high motives of these persons, I urge them nevertheless to consider the findings mentioned above.

Chapter 12

Why History?

In meeting social revolution, why bother with history? Do we not know by its face what is right and wrong? Perhaps. But many Quakers now have gone farther than to know the difference. More and more, we are analyzing the structure of society and how it may be changed, so that wrong will be made right by structure, not just case by case. I turned to history because I needed to know how the structures have evolved, and how they have changed in the past.

Quaker thought and action were simpler in an earlier age. When our religion was founded in the middle of the seventeenth century, Quakers tried to avoid involvement in politics. They neither opposed authority nor favored it. The English civil war, two Dutch wars, the Spanish war, the Thirty Years' War, the War of Devolution, and the War of the League of Augsburg and Grand Alliance all involved England in the first half century of Quakerism. Yet Quakers - while they would not participate in those wars - neither debated their justice nor did anything to stop them. If the Quakers did lobby the politicians, it was usually to protect their own: Quakers persecuted for religious reasons.

Nor did early Quakers have formulas for poverty. Just one century before George Fox, Ket's Rebellion (1549) had protested the sheep enclosures, by which village commons were divided among landowners, with the result that poor farmers were deprived of land on which to graze their cattle. Landholdings were becoming more consolidated in the hands of the rich. Those driven off the land had been forced into cities, where they sought employment in such numbers that Queen Elizabeth (r.1558-1603) had been required to strengthen the poor laws and call on the parishes for help. In the following (seventeenth) century, Diggers and early Levellers* - but not Quakers - tore down the hedges that deprived the poor of the commons. Their poverty was greatly exacerbated by the civil war that raged in the very decade that Quakerism was founded. Quakers spoke out against poverty and war, but they had no political program to resolve them.

Indeed, when John Lilburne, leader of the revolutionary Levellers - disillusioned, flogged, imprisoned, starved, and beaten for his attempts to establish a new constitution to protect liberties and to bring rights to the poor - finally came to the Quakers for solace, he was shocked at their political aloofness. His biographer (Gregg 1961:343) writes of his astonishment:

> Lilburne was prepared to find humility and directness of speech in the Quakers, yet hardly for such an answer as he got to his opening question to Luke Howard. "I pray, sir, of what Opinion are you?" "None," answered Luke Howard. The reply was so unexpected to one used to contention that it struck Lilburne into silence. This was the first of many visits, and when Lilburne was granted liberty on parole he went to Quaker meetings in the town, where, again, he met with a perspicacity and directness of speech that bore into his spirit as no words had done since the thunderings of Gouge and Sibbes twenty years earlier. On one occasion as he left a meeting, still without the full realization of

---

*There were two Leveller movements, one in the first decade of the seventeenth century, which spoke out against enclosures, and that of John Lilburne, simultaneous to the founding of Quakerism, which defended private property.

conversion, the speaker, George Harrison, ran after him, exclaiming, "Friend, Thou are too high for Truth!"

Such a rebuke, to one whose whole life had been active on behalf of the poor, in defiance of authority - whether it be that of the king, of the Courts, of Cromwell, of the Presbyterians who dominated Parliament, or of the Rump after Pride's Purge - would astound Quakers of today.

The activism of seventeenth-century Quakers was devoted almost single-mindedly to freedom of religion and to the suffering in prison of those who had been religiously persecuted. Quakers did make themselves offensive to others. They usurped pulpits, speaking not against the religion of the "steeplehouses" they had invaded but against its monopoly, its claim to sole Truth. They held protest meetings in churchyards against the services taking place within.

These protests were simple, in the directness of the issue. Monopoly religion, which saw only one way of Truth, was wrong, and Quakers would speak against it, suffer imprisonment against it, and alleviate the sufferings of their martyrs.

They did not tackle complex matters. They were not concerned whether the English or the Dutch should exclude each other from trading rights. In an attitude resembling "render unto Caesar," they cared little whether the Stuart monarchy was restored in 1660, even though they suffered from its religious persecution thereafter. They did not debate the navigation acts, nor did they protest the monopoly of the Merchant Adventurers or the colonialism - even the wars - of the East India Company. An agricultural revolution was about to take place - and historians have often said that it would have been impossible without the enclosures, which had so hurt the poor - but Quakers, not taking a side, had no need to join the issue.

The eighteenth century is called a period of quietism, when our spiritual ancestors tended their religion, themselves, and their separateness from the world. Once again the issues were simple: the conduct of meetings, dress style, marriage, exclusion of those who would not conform. The impact on the outside world was slight. Quakers of today speak little of that century; it is not one of which we are proud.

But it was also the century of John Woolman. His issue, too, was simple and direct: slavery was wrong; Indian land laws were wrong; it was wrong to sell rum to Indians. Wearing simple garments, traveling by foot where he could, he preached his doctrine to Quakers, persuading many communities to oppose slavery and individuals to free their slaves. He refused to buy the products of slavery. While I might question his paternalism on Indian rum or whether his boycott helped or harmed the slaves, nevertheless to him the questions were direct: these things were wrong; he would eschew them for himself and speak against them to others.

Slavery became the big issue of the nineteenth century. England had already freed its slaves and had declared the end of slavery in its empire in 1833. Quakers participated in the underground railroad in the United States, to harbor escaped slaves in "safe houses," so they might be taken to freedom in Canada. To others slavery might have been a complex issue, but to our spiritual ancestors this difference between right and wrong required no heavy reasoning. Nor was there any question that those being helped sought the help and wanted it just the way the Quakers provided it.

Opposition to war has always been a hallmark of Friends. Quakers opposed the Napoleonic wars and the Crimean War and helped alleviate the suffering of the enemy where they could, making themselves unpopular for that (Russell 1979:380; Brayshaw 1953: 287). At the outbreak of World War I, some Quakers joined ambulance units, some rejected war completely, some joined the army. While Quakers debated the rightness and wrongness of war, we did not as a society debate the issues of the war. Conscientious objectors took our stand because war was wrong, not because the Americans or French or British or Germans were wrong. Even before the war had ended, the American Friends Service Committee was founded on the simple issue of hunger. Quakers did not ask whether Germany had wanted to rule Europe or whether German soldiers had cut off the hands of Belgian children. The issue was simple: hungry people should be fed.

World War II was more complex. The Germans had overrun Europe in ways they did not dream of during World War I; torture, hunger, and intense suffering swirled in their wake. Many Quakers joined the army. To others, however, the question was still simple. While we did not condone German atrocities, the peace testimony was absolute.

After the war, the question was one of rebuilding Europe. Quakers were there in force, in work camps, in neighborhood houses to return a semblance of normal life to battered communities, and in other efforts of peace. The issue again was simple, even if twofold. Europe had to be rebuilt physically, but spiritually as well. Quakers wanted to show that we did not hate. The expression, "See what Love can do," comes from William Penn's writing, *Fruits of Solitude*, in 1693.

Immediately after World War II, Quakers attacked racial injustice. We supported the desegregation of schools. We sat with black friends in racially segregated restaurants until we were served. In the 1960s, we marched with Martin Luther King and sang "We shall overcome" with him in Washington. The trend away from simple protest had begun. The Friends Committee on National Legislation became the first organized Quaker lobby. Its founder, Raymond Wilson, stated its purpose as follows:

> That better world of tomorrow will not come just by wishing for it. It is incumbent upon the individual not only to try to be good, but also, individually and in concert with others, to try to be effective (FCNL Washington Newsletter, January 1982).

This simple statement marks a fundamental change in Quaker social action. Instead of being only conscientious objectors, in the 1960s Quakers tried - for the first time in our history - to *stop* a war. Instead of just marching side by side with blacks protesting Apartheid, although we have done that also, some of us have joined boycotts intended to change American and South African laws. Instead of just refusing to participate in war in Central America, some of us actively have tried to stop American participation in that war.

It is not that the issues have become more complex. Apartheid is just as wrong as slavery was or as racial discrimination has been in the United States. War in Central America is just as wrong as the English civil war. But when we go beyond protesting war and religious persecution, beyond feeding the hungry and freeing the slaves, and try the multifarious task of righting wrongs all over the world, be they economic, social, or political; when we do things that affect the lives of others, yet the others have not been - indeed, could not be - consulted, then we must be cautious - very cautious. We must know history, know economics, know governments, know how businesses function, and reason in complex ways in which we never have had to reason before.

Chapter 13

Slavery

I once read an article about Africa, "where religion is more about joy than guilt, where the wounds of black-white violence and tribal genocide are healed by . . . the Africans' short memory of hate" (Harden 1986:25). I thought long and hard about a religion filled with joy and not ridden with guilt, and I thought about the Africans. Are we guilty of destroying societies and economies in that beautiful continent by the slavery of our ancestors? We are guilty, but is our guilt unique? Does it matter whether it is unique?

Slavery and empires have existed from time immemorial. There is no historical record of a society in which they did not exist, in one form or another, until slavery was consciously abolished, and empires dismantled, by industrialized nations.

We sometimes hear of primitive tribes living in harmony, with equality because in the simple life there is no means to distinguish rich from poor and because clans formed "safety nets" for the poor. But this nostalgic vision has long been disproved by archaeologists. Tombs and mounds, and cities reconstructed by aerial photography, reveal great disparities of wealth and power thousands of years ago. Even if land existed sufficiently for subsistence, ancient peoples constantly thought that "others had better," so they migrated and conquered. Conquered people were sold as slaves. Walled cities and other fortifications in ancient times reveal how tribes and clans fought each other. Gold, obsidian, cattle, and housing distinguished rich from poor.

volcanic glass similar in composit'n to granite

We know of no era, and probably no place, in which slaves were not captured and cruelly treated.

Did Western capitalism bring slavery? No, slavery existed long before Western capitalism. Although money and wage labor were known in ancient Egypt, Mesopotamia, the Graeco-Roman world, and China, nevertheless the principal means of obtaining non-family labor was through slavery. Even when farming was the major activity, tribal élites would require women and slaves to do it, while they themselves were off at war.

Slavery and warfare have been known in Africa as long as anyone from outside has known Africa. When Arabs first penetrated south of the Sahara, around 1000 A.D., they found a great empire, known as Ghana, composed of dominant tribes which had conquered and enslaved others. As Berber tribes became converted to Islam, they began a concerted holy war (*jihad*) against the pagans of the desert. The Almoravid movement toppled the Empire of Ghana in the thirteenth century. The vacuum was quickly filled by a new Empire of Mali, which subjected neighboring peoples, among them the Songhai, and expanded into their territories.

In the fifteenth century, the Songhai revolted against their overlords, forming their own empire, reducing other peoples, capturing slaves, and demanding tribute from the conquered. In 1591, troops of the sultan of Morocco used muskets to reduce the Songhai, who were still armed with spears and bows and arrows. Europeans who later visited the capitals of the African empires reported walled cities, broad highways, hierarchical societies with privileges and wealth for the upper groups, government bureaucracies for efficient armies and taxation, poor people and slaves to do the work, and almost constant warfare - all this before "capitalism."

While the basic units of African society remained the clan and the tribe, these were mostly combined into kingdoms and empires either to conquer others or to defend themselves. There are some exceptions, for example pygmies in central Africa whose territories were too far into the forest to be of interest to others. Some "stateless peoples" managed to retain their independence until colonialization by the Europeans. But they are by far the minority. Some groupings, such as the Hausa states now in Nigeria (e.g., Katsina, Kano, Zaria), as well as Kebbi, Gobir, and Air, did not get beyond the stage of kingdoms.

But the following are a few of those that could truthfully be called empires, in that they subjected other peoples, conquered and colonized their lands, took slaves, and demanded tribute: Sokoto, a Fulani sultanate, Borno-Kanem, Ashanti, Dahomey, Oyo, Benin, the Pashalik of Timbuktu (under the Moroccans), the Bambara states, Kongo, Luanda, Luba, Loango, Lunda, Monomatapa, Butua, Nguni (or their subgroup, the Zulu), Madagascar, Luo, Baganda, Bunyoro, Kikuyu, Galla, Funj, Harar, Gondar, and Shoa (Amhara). Virtually all of Africa, possibly except some forest lands of the north-central interior, has been more or less continuously in the clutch of some empire, and by far the greatest portion of Africans either were slaves or held slaves or paid or received tribute to or from other Africans, as far back as the Arabs and the Europeans have known Africa and doubtless earlier.

The same is so for Indians in America, and especially so for the settled civilizations of Aztec, Maya, and Inca, all of which conquered and colonized other territories, enslaving their peoples.

All this was true *before* the world learned that it could increase its output by using capital. As capital became increasingly available and popular, at first the world gained its resources by the same methods it had used in the past: conquest and slavery. But in some parts of the world people began to perceive that these methods were inefficient. Capitalism required many people working together, some to produce some goods, others others; some to be traders, others financiers, and so on.

As the society became more complex, it was impossible to unite all these people by conquest and slavery. So they began to bargain with each other, to make contracts. Those parts of the world where the perception of voluntary cooperation and contract came first - northwest Europe and Japan - were the first to enjoy a sustained rise out of poverty. Contract feudalism, with unequal contracts at first, led to more and more contracts, less and less unequal, until feudalism had disappeared entirely. Westerners and Japanese have not gone as far along this path as they might, or as I hope they will, but they have taken the first steps.

As northwest Europeans began to see that trade outside their areas would bring people further away from poverty, they did a peculiar thing. In their relations with the rest of the world, they reverted to a condition they were abandoning at home - slavery. By 1500, few slaves remained in Europe. Yet the Europeans re-instituted slavery to remove Africans to the Americas. They themselves captured only a few slaves in Africa; for the most part, they bought them from willing African sellers, who perceived new opportunities for wealth through despoiling their neighbors.

Moral indignation against slavery had already arisen in the eighteenth century. Only in the nineteenth century did Europeans and their American descendants become aware that it did not benefit them as conquerors. Country by country, they outlawed slave trade by their own citizens: Denmark in 1803, Britain in 1807, the United States in 1808, Sweden in 1813, the Netherlands in 1814, and France in 1818. In 1833, the British outlawed the slave trade in the entire Empire and began enforcing the ban even on non-British ships. Why? A reasonable conjecture: they found that slave wars interfered with what they now considered legitimate trade for commodities.

Some believe that slavery ended in the United States because of the War between the States; some argue that slavery ended because it was not profitable to the plantations; economists disagree on whether this was so. But I think that slavery ended because, from a total social viewpoint, not just a plantation viewpoint, it was not profitable. Moral pressure speeded the process. Businesses became aware that free wage labor did not work well alongside a slave system. In 1802, the Prussian minister Leopold von Schrotter wrote that "serfdom and true industry are clear contradictions. Serfdom does not exist in any country in which agriculture and manufacturing prosper" (Kriedte 1983:112).

This awareness is especially revealed in Brazil, where slavery was abolished in 1888 mainly because free European laborers were reluctant to immigrate to a place where they would compete with slaves. That slavery could end without a war is testified by its peaceful demise in all of Europe and in all the American countries except the United States and Sainte Domingue (Haiti). Reform can come nonviolently. Europeans, who did not initiate the slavery in Africa, were the ones to end it. Their motive was profit. The profit motive can bring good things.

We did commit slavery and other heinous crimes. We have a reason to be guilty but also a right to be proud. In the few centuries from the industrial revolution to the present, the disparities in income and wealth that have existed from time immemorial have begun to narrow, relatively if not absolutely. We have a long way to go, but we are on the way. How slavery was ended in the past will help us understand how injustices may be resolved in the future.

Chapter 14

The Massive Chasm

In this chapter I address the main historical reasons for the massive chasm: the wealth of the West and the poverty of the Third World. Other scholars will disagree with me, and I lay no claim to the sole truth. Rather, I tell of my perceptions: what I have seen in history that has led me to the beliefs I hold. I limit myself to major forces and omit many qualifications, subreasons, and explanations that would be essential if this were a scholarly treatise.

In simple terms, I believe that the keys to material well being for everyone lie in pluralist societies, with decentralization and dispersion of power. They lie also in the creation of institutions of trust, mutual accountability, and peaceful bargaining. War and the excesses of power are the principal hindrances.

As early as 1000 A.D., Europe and Japan were becoming societies of many corporate groups, hereafter "pluralist societies." Each group, with its own internal structure, bargained with other groups on behalf of its members. In Europe, the groups were village farmers, lords of the land, merchants, traders, high government officials, local officials, the pope, clerics, town patricians, princes, kings, military officers, and on and on. As time went on, new groups evolved: craft guilds, labor unions, Levellers, Diggers, Quakers, political parties, League of Women Voters, the Sierra Club, and many more. An analogous set arose in Japan: emperors, shoguns, Buddhist monks, azukari dokoro, jito, ikki, samurai, possessors of different shiki, daimyo, and so on. It is not necessary to translate all these terms, only to suggest that they served a similar purpose to the groups emerging in Europe.

By bargaining and successive contracts, the rules by which different groups would respect each other evolved slowly in each place. Lower-ranking groups would lever their power upward, by alliances with higher-ranking. Suppose town patricians and lords of the manor rivaled each other for, say, trade privileges. Suppose they were equally matched, neither able to gainsay the other. By allying with one or the other of these stronger groups, peasants could tip the balance.

In *The Story of Land*, I refer to this process as "the peasants applying leverage" when they had little power. Repeatedly they levered their power upward, in both Europe and Japan, shifting their alliances cleverly as the way opened, but always demanding a price. That price was usually improved conditions: security of tenure, lower rents and taxes, decrease in service obligations, or greater attention of town patricians and lords to their needs.

Trust

The institutions developed to monitor these agreements, such as courts, markets, and village councils, brought with them trust. As people came to expect certain behavior from others, they came to trust them.

Take, for example, paper currency. Why did European monarchs not issue paper currency in the twelfth century? Probably because no one would trust it. But as trade expanded, more money was needed than could be supplied by gold and silver mines. So Europeans began to use promissory notes (IOUs) as currency. These would pass from hand to hand, collecting endorsements, sometimes twenty or thirty, along the way, until the notes fell due.

Because notes could not always be trusted, they were laden with restrictions. Endorsement from one merchant to another required witness by a notary. If the initial debtor defaulted, the holder could not instantly claim value from any endorser. He had to find them, not always an easy task, in a certain order. Law courts in Paris could not enforce obligations in Lyons. So promissory notes, although useful in supporting trade, were not an efficient currency.

But over time, with greater predictability of behavior, therefore greater trust, these restrictions were eased. By the seventeenth century in England and Holland, promissory notes signed by reliable merchants passed as easily as money does today. Merchants, later goldsmiths, still later banks, and finally governments began to issue them as money, and lo and behold, paper money *that could be trusted* was born. Not always trusted, for inflation-minded monarchs abused it as governments do today, but still a significant advance.

Some will say: trust others and they will trust you. This is a noble thought, but history tells me otherwise. Only after bargains are made with great caution and some mistrust; only after they are nonetheless kept over the years because it is mutually advantageous to keep them; only then does trust arise. When trust is offered gratuitously, it is often violated. If we wish the Russians and the Americans to trust each other, we must not rely on idealistic notions about trust, but we must know how trust has arisen in the past.

I now submit that pluralism, fluid and changing alliances, use of leverage to enhance power through alliances, bargains that were unequal at first, institutions, and trust are the main reasons why wealth, power, and income have increased and tended toward greater equality in both the West and Japan. Poor and rich rise together; they are partners more than adversaries. Economic development requires cooperation among large numbers of people, many of whom do not know each other and often are half way around the world from each other. They must work together through trusted modes of behavior.

Accountability

In virtually the entire world before the tenth century, power and wealth were private. The monarch was an enterpriser like the merchant. Mainly, the monarch and merchant both inherited their jobs from their fathers. The monarch sold "his" people defense and legal protection. Except when they revolted, the people had no choice but to buy these services at the price he set, known as taxes. He paid "his" army and "his" judges the way the merchant would pay his employees or buy his materials. With no legal distinction between the individual and his office, the concept of a public treasury separate from the private purse did not exist. Tax moneys belonged to the king as a person. He had to provide the contracted services, but he was accountable to no one for his money.

Jobs in medieval governments also belonged to the monarch, as private property. He would sell them, for either a lump sum or a long-term rent. So buyers would invest in government jobs the way a merchant invests in capital. The proceeds for being tax collector or judge generally belonged to the officeholder, except as he had agreed to pay them, like rent, to higher authority. Often the monarch granted land, of which he was sovereign-by-conquest, to civil servants, and their pay was what they could extort from the serfs living upon it. A whole hierarchy of officials thus emanated from king, pope, sultan, or Chinese emperor. At the bottom of the pile were slaves, owned as property; serfs attached to the land although with some legal rights; and freemen, who generally owned no property.

It has been the great accomplishment of the West and Japan to break this system: to define public service as distinct from private property; to convert governors from owners of rights into public servants; to separate the public purse from bureaucrats' private funds; to institute impartial justice; and to demand accountability for public funds.

Only a pluralist society could do this. Only by successive bargaining among the groups did the upper classes gradually relinquish their authority. We have not accomplished this completely, but compared with the rest of the world, the West is well on its way. The story is well told in history. In England, major thresholds were the Parliaments of Edward I (r.1272-1307); and the civil war and its aftermath (1642-1688), in which Parliament beheaded one king, invited back his son, and deposed another, thus proving itself superior to the monarch. The story is also told in the maturing of the law, the banking system, and a government bureaucracy with checks and balances.

We all compare accomplishment with tasks undone, but we may place different values on each. If we perceive accomplishment clearly and remaining tasks dimly, we become euphoric, waving the flag and telling of our wondrous democracy. We may not see how minority groups still do not know equal justice or equal opportunity. But if we ignore accomplishment and focus only on present injustices - racism, militarism, cruelty, and poverty - we lose our self-esteem and wallow in the guilt of not having completed the task. Let us place both accomplishment and remaining tasks in perspective, so we can be proud of what we have done even as we gird our forces for the struggle that lies ahead.

The Third World

Some say that the West is more developed because we stole our resources from the Third World through slavery, colonialism, and unfair prices. This I heard again and again from my students in Bolivia and Mexico, and I continue to hear it from intellectuals who constitute the governments of champions. These arguments might be plausible had not *all* the world engaged in slavery - the West and Third World alike - including Sub-saharan Africa before it knew about Europe; had not most areas of the world been colonies in one way or another, including the United States; and had resources correlated with economic development.

But wealth, stolen or otherwise, hinders economic advancement more than it promotes it. Spain and Portugal, the European countries that most despoiled Africa, took most slaves and carted back to Europe most of the riches of the New World, became the least developed in western Europe. If wealth brought economic development, Saudi Arabia and Kuwait would be among the most developed today. We saw in chapter 13 that African countries were among the greatest despoilers of each other. Spanish and Portuguese overlords in the Americas cruelly bled the Indians. If we theorize that despoiling others brings economic advancement to the exploiters, we would reason that Africa and Latin America, governed by their élites, would be among the most developed areas today.

Why, then, is the Third World so economically backward? I believe for all the following reasons: power is still private; often the public and the private purses flow together; the law is not uniform or impartial; no pluralist society emerged. Ethnic groups continue to fight each other. Groups did not learn sufficiently to bargain with each other, nor the poorer ones to lever their power, holding overlords accountable for the use of national resources. Mutual mistrust prevented people from issuing promissory notes or starting banks, except as Western money systems were imported. The rulers use the monetary system as private printing presses, sucking resources from the poor through inflation. The different groups do not cooperate adequately to lift themselves from poverty.

Ministers in Kenya presided with authority over meetings that I attended, not seeking the advice of their staffs but ordering them to do what they - in their superior wisdom - saw fit. I have seen the same in other African countries and throughout Latin America. If you read that sentence in an American context, you might think I am "griping." But the experience is not personal to me; it is the way the system works.

An economist named Clif Barton (1974) noticed, in Vietnam of the 1960s, that the manufacturing economy consisted of many, many firms of less than five employees, some with over 100 employees, and few in between. Such discontinuity is not natural, Barton reasoned. Why so few firms of between five and 100 employees?

Because, he concluded, where power is private, permission must be granted - and paid for - to undertake any venture. His hypothesis - not provable but logical - was that large firms could afford to pay officials for permission to do business. At the other pole, small firms were too poor for the officials to bother with. Medium-sized firms, however, commanded official attention but could not afford the payoffs. Therefore, either the middle-sized firms were milked out of existence or the small ones were reluctant to grow into visibility.

Let us not confuse this condition with Western concepts of corruption. Instead, it is a logical, well-coordinated system of private privilege. The legitimate right to receive payoffs is the private property of officials, which they may buy from higher officials. Such a system - much like Western feudalism ten centuries ago - is essential to social functioning in the Third World.

In Brazil it has a name, *jeito* (Rosenn 1984). Because it is costly to business enterprises, however, it is not compatible with economic development. Because it is based on privilege, it is not compatible with social justice. Multiply it by hundreds of institutions - the legal system, the banks, all government agencies from the president's office down to the village official - and any economic activity either becomes limited to family enterprise or, if big, becomes subject to costs too great to be competitive in world markets. So much of whatever is produced must be paid to officials that little is available for the poor.

But economic development and poverty are not simple questions, to be explained away with one simple reason such as *jeito*. War, plague, despoiling one's neighbor, slavery, serfdom, and other types of exploitation all help explain poverty and backwardness. Without these destructive social patterns, Europe might have had its industrial revolution in the thirteenth century instead of the eighteenth. Egypt might have waxed wealthy in the first century A.D.

Still, war, exploitation, and slavery cannot be the conditions producing the massive chasm because they were common to both the West and what is now the Third World before the chasm occurred. How *did* such differences come about?

Why did the West become characterized by pluralism, contract, and institutions of accountability and trust, while the Third World remained locked in authoritarianism, personalism, and private rights to positions of power? My studies of history tell me *how* the chasm occurred but not *why*. The West changed, by forming new groups, jockeying among them, making alliances, and using leverage in negotiation, while the old patterns of government by power, authority, and personality persisted in the Third World. "Why" is the problem with which I am now grappling. I think I have some ideas. While I talk them over with my students, they are not mature enough to write about. I am hoping to tell more in *The Horizon Society*.

The differences are not polar. Some of the characteristics I have attributed to the Third World are found in the West, and vice versa. But one set of characteristics is dominant in one area and the other in the other.

If I am now a conservative, it is only with respect to the West. I want to conserve the institutions that have been so laboriously fashioned. I want to build upon them and change them rather than let them be cast aside in revolution. I am *not* a conservative with respect to the Third World. The old institutions *must* change radically if justice for the poor will come about. But violent revolution will not change them; instead, it re-creates them in new guise. There is no shortcut to the tedious bargaining, interim failures, and slow fashioning of a pluralist society.

The next two chapters concern wealth: in land (Chapter 15) and in capital (Chapter 16). Wealth is too concentrated: too much belongs to the rich and too little to the poor. Some may say, "Well, take it from the rich and give it to the poor." How? Usually the prescription is to set up a government of champions who act on behalf of the poor. Can it be done any other way?

John Locke, the eighteenth-century advocate of private property, was of a different mind. Remembering England's feudal history, he opposed concentration of property in king and lords, and his answer was to disperse ownership. From the end of the nineteenth century on, the ownership of wealth and income in England and the United States has moved in the way Locke would have wanted: more widespread and much less concentrated. This movement toward greater equality has been strong but not continuous. There have been setbacks, such as an alarming one in the past decade. But we have always returned to the trend. Let us conserve that trend. If we are on the right track, let us not turn around just because we haven't reached our goal.

Chapter 15

Land

"Property is theft," declared Pierre-Joseph Proudhon, socialist of the early nineteenth century. Do we have the right to own any property at all? Yes, we do, said Proudhon. Have the rich and powerful stolen property from the poor and weak? Yes, many times. Let us examine these questions.

Who owns the land? This question more than any other undergirds the revolutions in El Salvador and Nicaragua. Our consciences are pricked as we recall how powerful people have seized land from the poor: throughout Latin America in the Spanish and Portuguese conquests; in the United States as our ancestors hemmed in the Indians; in Africa as colonial rulers confiscated farmland. Does justice require that all this land should be given back?

The answer is a qualified Yes. But first, let us examine two widespread beliefs:

(1) that a landed oligarchy is politically powerful in many third-world countries, including Chile, El Salvador, and Nicaragua under Somoza. This oligarchy, which controls the government and the army, obdurately resists returning the land to the Indians from whom they stole it.

(2) that the Government of the United States supports such an oligarchy.

I believe neither of these assertions is true.

First belief: the landed oligarchy

In our research for *The Peasant Betrayed*, we quickly perceived that despite some exceptions - such as Guatemala - the old landed oligarchy is politically weak. Taking land from the oligarchs is, in fact, quite easy. Wars to take it have been brief, but mostly it has been taken without wars.

Why? Probably for the same reasons that landholders were weak in Europe in the nineteenth century and Japan in the twentieth: because of the rise of manufacturing and trade. A quarter of a century ago, most people in the Third World worked on farms. But in country after country manufacturing has grown at annual rates of 4% or so; 7% to 10% are common. By 1983, the latest year for which I have comprehensive data, the populations of more than half the Latin American countries were over 50% urban: 83% in Argentina; 78% in Brazil; 74% in Colombia; 50% in Ecuador; 50% in El Salvador; 68% in Mexico; 55% in Nicaragua; 56% in Panama; 66% in Peru; 84% in Uruguay; and 71% in Venezuela (IADB 1984:415). Urbanization has proceeded in Asia and Africa as well.

Thus a new political group has arisen - manufacturers and merchants - whose interests conflict abruptly with the landed oligarchy. This new group wants cheap food for its workers, but old tenure forms, such as the hacienda, cannot supply it. Believing that landowning peasants would produce more efficiently and therefore sell for less, the urban classes are swinging over to reform. Serious reforms - which took the lands of the oligarchy - have occurred all over the world. Among those which followed a non-socialist pattern, the best known in Latin America are in Bolivia, Chile before Allende, Mexico, Peru, and Venezuela.

So why all the fuss over land reform? The fuss is not over whether, but over who will control. In chapter 9, I suggested that the state wants farm profits, which it takes away from the landed oligarchy and does not give to the peasant. In countries of great struggle between Left and Right, each side wishes to control the land reform. Whoever controls the land controls the food supply, extorts the profits of agriculture, and rules the country.

Second belief: the United States and the landed oligarchy

Although our government does not speak with one voice - often it is muddled and confused - enough politicians have grasped that the landed aristocracy is a dying class, so they do not want us to ally ourselves with them. But our government also shows no compassion for the peasant. Rather, it is a partner of the Right in its attempt to keep the land from the Left. It has urged land reforms and supported them financially in Japan, Philippines, South Korea, and Taiwan. President Kennedy made land reform a plank of the Alliance for Progress, and the United States assisted in reforms in Bolivia, Brazil, Chile, Colombia, Costa Rica, Ecuador, El Salvador, Guatemala, and Venezuela. These reforms varied in their effectiveness - a few were indeed shams (Colombia, Ecuador, Guatemala) - but certainly the United States connived in expropriating substantial lands from the oligarchy in the others. It would brook no assistance to any land reform by the Left, however.

Reasons for the beliefs

Left and Right have each tried to deprecate the reforms of the other. Maybe you have heard that the United States proposes only "pretend" reforms in order to stave off "real" ones (propaganda of the Left). Or have you heard that the reforms of socialist governments are "made in Moscow" (propaganda of the Right)?

In Chapter 10 I told of *A Peasant of El Salvador*, the play that stereotyped Juan, the peasant. Much of the dialogue in this play is true: disappearances, murders, terror. But one scene presented a false image when it ridiculed Phase I of the Salvadoran government's land reform, which is supported by the United States. In the real case, within two months of announcing Phase I, the government had confiscated all estates above 250 hectares, striking a mortal blow at the oligarchy. These lands, which have not been returned, were made into peasant "cooperatives," amounting to 25% of El Salvador's cultivable surface. I know of no other land reform in any part of the world - not Allende's Chile, not China, not Cuba, not Mexico - which had confiscated such a large proportion of oligarchic land so promptly after the reform had been announced.

Shortly after Phase I had taken place in the play, *A Peasant of El Salvador*, Bishop Romero was depicted as saying, "When a dictatorship has so attacked human rights, when it becomes unbearable, all channels of dialogue are cut off, then the church may speak of your legitimate right to armed insurrection." In the real case, within two months after Phase I had been announced, the guerrillas had started the war. It seems to me that they might have waited, or offered to assist the government in implementing the reform, setting up ways to monitor it and enforce it, instead of launching into a war destined to kill thousands of people, undermine the livelihood of peasants, and destroy the national economy, justified only by their *belief* that the government would not keep its promise. It also seems to me inappropriate for the play to call for violent revolution when peaceful alternatives remained untried. It was *not true* that "all channels of dialogue (had been) shut off."

Four years after a large portion of oligarchic land had been expropriated in El Salvador, a publication by the American Friends Service Committee (AFSC) wrote as if it had never happened at all, and as if it couldn't happen (Berryman 1983:21):

> Not only has the land reform not worked - *it cannot work under the existing regime* [emphasis

> added]. To work it would have to provide access to land to a significant portion of the landless rural population, and in order to do that it would have to include a much larger area of agro-export land, that is, expropriate the oligarchy's landholdings.

Berryman based his charge on the fact that Phase II, which was to have expropriated middle-sized farms, mainly coffee, had not occurred. The government's explanation, which I consider valid, was that politically, it could not do everything at once. Once again, Mao, Castro, Allende and others took years to do as much as the Salvadoran government had done in two months. To say definitively that a land reform "cannot work under the existing regime," without comparing it with experiences elsewhere, is to me both a quick acceptance of the propaganda of the Left and a call for armed revolution.

While I hold no brief for the government's land reform, or that of the guerrillas either, if they ever tell us what it will be, nevertheless El Salvador confirms the proposition that the fuss over land reform is not one of whether, but of which side will control. No one could possibly conduct a land reform on such a battlefield as is found there now. With anarchy and chaos, individual interests and private armies have seized many of the smaller (Phase III) plots. The Left uses this fact to fuel its propaganda that the government's reform is a farce.

What kind of land reform?

Land has been stolen from the peasant, and it ought to be returned. The dilemma is not one of land reform, but of what kind.

I speak of land in the Third World, particularly in Latin America but also in Africa north of the Sahara and south of the Limpopo. I speak of land in India and Pakistan but not in the mountains of Burma or Thailand. I speak of land in

Vietnam and China but not in Taiwan or Japan. I do not propose returning land to Indians in the United States any more than I do to Celts in western Europe. We do not know from whom the Celts stole it. I would not give Texas and California back to Mexico, any more than I would give Mexico back to the tribes that the Aztecs and the Mayas enslaved. Virtually all land - wherever we are in the world - was at one time stolen by force. How far back must we go to determine its "rightful owner?" We must use our sense of what is fair and what is feasible.

Since land was given us by God, some have argued that it belongs to all the people; it should not be appropriated into private property. Engraved on the entrance to the Ministry of Education in Mexico are the words: *La tierra es de todos, como el aire, el agua, la luz, y el calor del sol* (land is for all, like air, water, light, and heat of the sun).

There are, however, a few problems. "All the people" cannot stand on a given piece of land. Nor can "all the people" build houses upon it or all cultivate it. Once the crop is in, "all the people" do not sit around a table to eat it. If these things are to be done on a given plot, they must be done by some and not by others. Who is to choose, and how?

When power over land is concentrated - whether in the old aristocracy or in a socialist state or a nonsocialist state - that power is abused and the peasant is robbed. The only solution I can see - and it is the one peasants have always wanted the world over - is to divide the land among the peasants in private property. I cannot supply the specifics for every case, but in general the land should be given to the farmer who tills the soil, whatever may have been his or her previous type of tenancy. Whether the landowner should be compensated is a local-specific question, depending on which way will most avoid violence, promoting compromise and good feelings among those who must cooperate thereafter.

Yet this formula does not describe the land reforms of Chile, China, Cuba, Egypt, El Salvador, Nicaragua, Tanzania, or most others. So how will it come about? If history is any guide, it will come about only through leverage: when the peasant negotiates for it from strength, and when he or she joins powerful allies such as businesspeople who find it in their interest to help. It will not be given "graciously" by any government, domestic or foreign, socialist or nonsocialist, or by you or me.

For the peasant, this takes time. Sadly, land reform is like growing up. If you try to do it all at once, you only postpone further the day that it really happens.

Chapter 16

Capital and Profits

If land should be widely distributed and held in private property, what of capital?

What would you think of a society in which the ownership of industry and agriculture (hereafter, capital) were widespread, so that few people were very rich and few very poor? Each person would receive a wage for his or her own work, plus the profit arising from that person's share of the nation's capital. Stocks of some industries would be owned by a social insurance fund, whose profit would be used for retirement benefits, health and unemployment insurance, and welfare, no questions asked, for those who cannot work. Hereafter, I will say "social insurance" to cover all these. The profits might not be large enough to pay all health bills, but they would certainly do so for those who could not afford them otherwise.

That is my ideal society. It possesses one diametric difference from our current society, in which the government serves as intermediary for social insurance. At present, income and profits are taxed by government, and government pays the social insurance. In my ideal society, by contrast, government would be canceled out. It might manage the fund or contract it to private insurance companies which would in turn be government-insured, but the people at large would own it. In technical jargon, the assets would be *vested* in them. A certain portion of the nation's capital would *belong* to the retired and the poor in the form of insurance policies, from which they would have the legal right to be paid if they met certain conditions, such as unemployment, age, and sickness, just the way an insured homeowner has the legal right to collect if his or her house burns down.

In our present society, the socially insured have no vested rights in government funds at all; they depend totally on government's goodwill and financial capacity. Despite a worker's payment of social security for all his or her working life, Congress and the President may decrease the retirement benefit if they wish or take it away entirely if they dare. They have indeed reduced Medicare and have threatened the same for social security.

In a communist state, the socially insured also depend totally on the goodwill and financial capacity of the government. If the government squanders business profits or tax revenues on war, as both our own government and that of the Soviet Union are now doing, less remains for the socially insured.

Would my ideal society change your attitude toward profit? Some think of "profit" and "greed" in the same breath. But *generically*, profit is simply the return on capital, with no value judgment placed upon it. If the nation's ownership of capital is unevenly divided, so that a few people receive most of the profit, then we are right to think of greed. But in my ideal society, profit would feed the poor, insure the unemployed, and pay pensions. Then perhaps we would not associate it with greed.

Let us examine generic profit. Suppose Robinson Crusoe, upon his island, has no tools. He picks fruit and catches fish with his hands. But when he makes a fishing rod (capital), he catches more. Let us say that the food he gathers without his rod is "real wages," produced by his labor alone. If he works the same number of hours using the rod, the *extra* catch is "real profit," attributable to the rod, which is capital. This is the way economists assign responsibility for the nation's product between labor and capital.*

We face a contradiction on profit and greed. On the one hand, we think of high profit-seekers as greedy. But on the other hand, profit-seeking reduces waste, which we cannot afford.

Too many people are hungry, so we must use our capital to produce the most we can. Therefore, every piece of capital (every machine or building) and potential capital (machines that might be made or buildings that might be built) must be made the most productive possible. I don't want to go too far on this, because "the most possible" may not be the most practical. I just want to engender the idea of husbanding our resources well and using them wisely. To do so, capital must be invested where it is most profitable, because there it produces the most goods and services. Robinson would make a net or a rod, whichever produced more fish (greater profit).

Perhaps our mental dilemma comes because we may think of profit and wages as opposites: the more the profit, the less the wage. Greed causes capitalists to pay the lowest wages possible, in order to earn the highest profits. They do this, any chance they get. But in the aggregate, they cannot do it. Historically, in order to earn greater profit, businesspeople have had to pay higher wages. *Thus the rate of real profit (percentage of profit over investment) has remained remarkably constant over two centuries in the United States, while the rate of real wages (dollars per hour) has continuously risen.*

---

*"Real wages" and "real profit" mean the goods and services that money wages and money profit, respectively, can buy. Since Robinson does not have money, his wages and profit are real to begin with.

Why? Because the real world is more complicated than Robinson Crusoe's island. Labor could produce little without tools and machines, but with them it produces immensely. Therefore, it might seem that real wages, the physical product of labor alone, would be low, and real profit, the increment when machines are added, high.

Not so. As businesses bid labor away from each other in competition, they offer higher and higher wages. In the industrialized West and Japan, therefore, *more and more of the increment of earnings created by capital has gone to wages instead of to profits*. That is why wages are now about 70% of the U.S. national income and profits only about 30%, whereas profits commanded a much greater share a century ago. Thus the paradox, that when we increase our capital, wage rates go up but the rate of profit does not.*

I believe that my ideal society may indeed be the one we are approaching: the "horizon society," though I cannot say for sure until I do more research. Yet with respect to social insurance, did I not say it is diametrically opposed to our present society? Now I must modify that. We have many private pension plans and group health insurance to supplement social security, and these are increasing. Whereas few private plans existed half a century ago, in 1983, out of a total civilian work force of 108.5 million, 47.1 million, or 43.4%, were covered by private pension plans, and 66.2 million, or 61.0%, by group health plans (USDC 1986:421). The government *cannot* tap these funds to feed its defense budget the way it can social security.

---

*We are now touching upon, but not entering, the marginal theory of income distribution, propounded by the Austrian school of economists in the mid-nineteenth century. Under this theory - for reasons too complex to explain here and which my students do not always understand even after a whole semester - the value of the national product becomes fully attributed, in precise proportions, to the factors (land, labor, capital) that produced it.

How widespread is stockholding in the United States? Not very, but increasingly. Whereas in 1959, 12.5 million individuals held stock, or 7.1% of the population of 176.6 million, the figure for 1983 was 42.4 million, or 18.7% of the population of 226.5 million (USDC 1974:466; 1986:5,509). While we have a long way to go before 100% of the people own shares in the nation's capital directly, we are at least moving in that direction.

How much are corporate profits? For the fifteen years from 1970 through 1984, these averaged an annual net return on investment, including both dividends and interest paid and undistributed profits, of 10.4% before taxes and 7.2% after taxes (USDC 1986:523). But these rates apply to all companies. Suppose we take only the 500 largest industrial corporations. In 1983, the net return on stockholder equity was 10.7% and in 1984, 13.6%. If capital gains to stockholders are added to the net income, of course the return varies widely; the market goes up and down. In 1983, for the 500 largest, it was 30.2%, and in 1984 a loss of 0.8% (USDC 1986:533). To me, these rates are not excessive, and I do not look upon corporate profits as gouging the economy.

But there is more to be done than to let present trends continue. Private pension plans may multiply and numbers of stockholders increase, and still the poor may be left out. Some social action is necessary to bring every individual into a meaningful plan. The plans must have minimum standards, to provide adequate income and insurance. These standards - it seems to me - must be set by government. If protection is to be complete, against bankrupted insurance companies for example, the private plans must also be government-guaranteed. There is precedent for this in the guarantee of bank deposits.

So, how has my own thinking evolved on capital?

First, I try not to think of profits and greed as necessarily going together. Sometimes they do, but not always. Profits are certainly not enormous. They are unevenly divided, and they make some people rich. But think of the potential! Generically, profits are merely part of the increment of welfare from machines and technology. With improved social organization, we can use them positively.

Second, I am encouraged by trends under way, toward more people owning stock, and therefore more widespread enjoyment of profits. Let us expand private pension and insurance plans, which will also own stock, vested in their members. Although widely owned private plans are more secure for the worker - government cannot take them away - let us not phase out government social insurance until everyone is covered privately. Furthermore, private plans should be insured by government so that no poor person will lose by having chosen an improvident or unlucky private insurer.

Third, private pension plans will probably not, by themselves, encompass the poor. Only the employed contribute to them. It is here that government action will be necessary, to provide pension plans and health and unemployment insurance for the poor. These might be financed out of taxes, like our present social security and unemployment insurance. Unlike our present system, however, the proceeds would buy shares in industry instead of government securities.

Fourth, I propose that widespread private ownership of capital serves the same social purposes, of greater equality and protection, falsely attributed to communism. Like each plot of farmland, each industry cannot be administered by "all the people," nor is its product divided among "all the people." Instead, communism concentrates the management of vast amounts of capital in a small number of people, who are not held accountable for their trust. In my ideal society, by contrast, many, many individuals, in many, many places, would share in managing, or in choosing the managers, of our nation's wealth. Some companies might be big, if they need to be for greatest efficiency, but the power of bigness would be dispersed through widespread ownership.

Finally, this chapter raises a host of problems that would have to be addressed, and this book is not big enough. Private pension plans may be politically manipulated; corporations are not necessarily managed fairly just because stockholding is diverse; and pension funds will be fraudulently diverted unless carefully guarded. Also, once we have widespread participation in both land and capital, how will we maintain it? I have not gone into all the checks and balances, all the social agreements, to be achieved by negotiation, bargaining, and compromise. I have only raised a general concept, whose reality would be hammered out by the many participating groups.

Chapter 17

The System and the People

When I was a child, my Sunday School teacher taught me to say: "And Jesus increased in wisdom and stature, and in favor with God and man" (Luke 2:52). The implication was clear. I should do likewise. I was lord of my own behavior and responsible for it.

Gradually, however, I learned about "the system." The system was a way of doing things that eclipsed my own will, forcing behavior upon me. As a child, I presumed it was benevolent, made by wise people to lead us into righteousness. Only with World War II and conscription did I begin to question that. Suppose my Light was different from what the system required?

I began to think of the system as a private club whose members were beings but not necessarily people. Each one had arms, legs, one body, and one brain. One being was called "the United States," another "Britain," another "United States Steel," another "the military," and so on. They would talk to each other, sometimes fight with each other, but they made up rules for us mortals. If I could no longer decide for myself what was right and wrong, how could I grow in wisdom and stature?

My first serious move to buck the system came as a conscientious objector in World War II. The fact that I would do so caused me to see the system differently. It became both benevolent and malevolent, but in each case it had no mind of its own. I learned that no one can force me to do anything I do not want to do, so long as I am prepared to take the consequences.

On the benevolent side, the system is a set of social arrangements agreed upon, one by one, by our ancestors and ourselves. Each one appeared advantageous when it was adopted. As the system developed, it did foreclose earlier opportunities. In some parts of our country, it is no longer possible to earn the same living on a small farm that our ancestors did. Modern methods and capital have so reduced the price of food that only on a modern farm, with greater production per person-hour, can one earn a living wage. The simple manufactures bought by our ancestors are no longer available.

But the new goods and new methods came incrementally: piped water, inside toilets, milking machines, hybrid seed, tractors and harvesters. These made food cheaper for poor and rich alike. They made it possible to feed a growing population that has outstripped the potential of small farms. Each innovation was accepted voluntarily by many people. No corporate mind forced us into any changes. We could even undo the system, piece by piece, the same way we set it up. But we are unwilling to "go back" because we like the system for the same reasons that our ancestors chose it. It limits our behavior because we must get along with others, in ways that help us all.

But the system is also malevolent, for two reasons. First, those who agreed upon it were human, error-prone. They might legitimize war to solve international disputes, but they would be wrong. Second, the system was not always made by agreement. Parts were forced by the powerful upon the weak: slavery and colonialism, for example.

Evil though these forces were, they also cannot be blamed on a corporate mind. The captains of illegal slave ships, who, when pursued by the British, threw their human cargo overboard rather than be caught with it, were human beings who made those decisions themselves. "The system" might have justified them, but the responsibility was theirs.

Marx condemned the behavior of the bourgeoisie but not the bourgeoisie themselves. He deemed them to be as much victims of the system as were the workers, for they were forced to act as the system directed. I find this thought dehumanizing, for it attributes a corporate mind to "the system," thus excusing individuals for our aberrations and our atrocities. I cannot accept any social descriptor that removes from me and from my fellow human beings the responsibility for our actions.

Today, when I hear stories of multinational corporations, I wonder if we conceive of some powerful being - a flaming dragon, perhaps - with a corporate mind? Remember the stereotypes we used to have of ethnic groups? Do we have similar stereotypes of members of the system? Do we think of all multinational corporations as behaving alike? Are their officials but arms and legs commanded by a super-brain? Or do we imagine groups of individuals with inner conflicts and inner lights, who may see the world differently from each other, capable of being reached and of reaching us?

If our first thought is to grow in wisdom and stature and in favor with God and man and woman, our way to change the system will reflect wisdom, stature, and favor. But if we are directed more toward the system itself than toward the people who comprise it; if we think in stereotypes and believe in corporate minds, we will tend to be coercive, violent. Then we will not learn the greatest lesson about the system, that it is nothing more than the way we change it.

Chapter 18

Liberation Theology, Revolution, and Sanctions

If we change the system by war, the new system is one of war. If we change the system by threat, we create a system of threat. If we change the system by love and compassion, we will live in a world of love and compassion.

If we change the system fast, by fiat, the new system will be overthrown fast, by fiat. But if we change the system slowly, patiently, compromisingly, plodding with each piece, our system will continue to change slowly, piece by piece.

We may be tempted by liberation theology, which speaks of oppression and calls for change in the name of religion. Some talk of this theology as one of peaceful change. More often, however, I have heard it in the context of military revolution and government by champion. Even the word "liberation" to me implies a violent wrenching away, as opposed to bargaining, pressure, and change by agreement. I have much to learn about liberation theology, but I will be cautious unless and until it manifests itself unequivocally in nonviolent form.

Violent revolution always returns the pre-existing society, only with different leaders in a different guise. Russian peasants were "liberated" in 1917 and allowed to invade the properties of their overlords. By 1933, all those properties had been taken by the state, with great bloodshed, and the peasant was as much a serf as before. In *The Peasant*

Betrayed, we have seen the same pattern in most modern land reforms of authoritarian governments. The Mexican Revolution - fought in the name of Land and Liberty, much like the Sandinista Revolution - created a new élite, which in recent years has violated the rights of Indians and has robbed the country of its capital and its industries, devastating the economy in the process.

The French Revolution - for Liberty, Equality, Fraternity - bankrupted the nation; it did little to redistribute property. It confiscated land from the nobility, then sold it back when the government ran out of funds. It launched Europe into catastrophic wars reverberating from Spain to Italy to Egypt to Holland to Austria to Russia, which did not die down until the defeat at Waterloo. After that, the monarchy was restored. The American Revolution left a nation similar to the one we had had before, but with different leaders. The subsequent history of the United States has paralleled that of Canada, which had no revolution.

Why does revolution re-create the old society? Because people have cultural attributes, forged by centuries of interaction. These attributes, unchanged by revolution, determine the society. The Third World - I have said before - is authoritarian. This is a simplified adjective, which conceals many qualifications of different circumstances, but basically it is true. Authoritarian societies are generally authoritarian at all levels: in empires, in national and local governments, in clans and tribes, and in families. Revolutionaries are just as authoritarian as the preceding oligarchy. Furthermore, authoritarian societies do not encourage economic development or social justice, whether they are led by Sandinistas or Somocistas or rulers of other name or breed.

In a pluralist society, however, peaceful change is not only possible, but built-in. Great social changes occurred in Europe and North America during the nineteenth century. The last vestiges of feudalism were wiped out - serfs liberated, lands distributed to peasants - in thirty-nine countries and princedoms, beginning with Savoy in 1771 and ending with Moldavia and Wallachia in 1864; only in France did the change come about by war (the Revolution) (Blum 1978:356). Other reforms included universal male suffrage (previously, property was a qualification; female suffrage came in the twentieth century); freedom from guild monopolies; universal education; and labor unions - all of them *peacefully* achieved.

Nor did the Revolutions of 1848 either speed up or slow down the process. In that year, country after country was convulsed in war, fought by an unlikely coalition of students in favor of more liberal education; nationalists wanting unification of Germany or Italy or freedom of Hungary from Austria; republicans wanting the end of monarchy (the French got rid of Louis-Philippe); businesses wanting freedom from government and guild monopolies; serfs and intellectuals wanting to end serfdom once for all and to distribute land of the nobles to its tillers; laborers wanting their unions recognized. All these reforms were demanded *at once*.

But violent revolution was crushed bloodily in country after country; leaders were hanged. France received a republic, but it lasted only four years. Hungarian independence was quashed by Austria. Labor unions were not recognized. Unification of Italy and Germany had to wait. No land reform, no peasant freedoms, resulted directly from 1848. But historian Priscilla Robertson (1952:412) tells us the sequel:

> Most of what the men of 1848 fought for was brought about within a quarter of a century, and the men who accomplished it were specific enemies of the 1848 movement. Thiers ushered in a third French Republic, Bismarck unified Germany, and Cavour, Italy. Deák won autonomy for Hungary within a dual monarchy; a Russian czar freed the serfs; and the

British manufacturing classes moved toward the freedoms of the People's Charter.

So the reforms were undertaken, peacefully, by the very people who had opposed them violently. They continued to come peacefully. Britain did not have a revolution in 1848, but it adopted roughly the same reforms as the Continent at roughly the same times or a bit earlier. Gladstone and Disraeli vied with each other for education and labor reform: Disraeli the Conservative, father of the Empire, brought liberal reform to Britain! Why are reforms initiated by Conservatives? Why did Nixon go to China?

I submit that social change has its own momentum, slow or slower, regardless of liberation theology, regardless of revolution, regardless of reforming or conservative governments. Violence neither brings social change nor stops it, though it may slow it down. We must find out the secret of social change: what *really* causes it? That is what I am working on, in my current research on *The Horizon Society*, which may last over the next ten years. I have hinted about what I think may be some of the causes, but of course my thoughts may change, and others may come forth with better ones in the meantime.

The concept of social change as accumulating a force of its own, which any individual can little influence, makes us revise our thinking toward our own behavior. Economic planning, liberation theology, revolutionary governments, and - yes - war, all are fraught with contradictions that we see but dimly. Rather than plot massive strategies, therefore, we must rely, step by step, on what is right. We must have faith that what is right will in the long run be effective, and what is wrong will not be.

This is the dilemma that many Friends, including myself, faced as conscientious objectors in World War II. We believed war was wrong, and we would not fight. As William Penn said:

A good end cannot sanctify evil means, nor must we ever do evil that good may come of it.

But suppose we find that by *not* doing harm, we are permitting grave consequences, not to ourselves but to others. Conscientious objectors in World War II knew about German atrocities against Jews, although we did not know until afterwards how grave the Holocaust had been. Were we justified in standing aside?

I faced a wrenching, agonizing decision in 1942: whether to lay aside a strategy for ending untold suffering by others, just because I considered the means immoral. The cool rationale for conscientious objection might have been that fighting World War II prolonged the *concept* of war, thus legitimizing the option for World War III. I believe that is so, and that is what I told others who demanded more than a moral reason. But it is not why I made the choice. I did so because and only because war is wrong.

I face the same moral choice today, on sanctions against South Africa. I do not know how to end the atrocities in South Africa any more than I knew how to end those in Germany. But it is wrong to deprive others of their livelihood, just as it is wrong to kill. We have taken reason as far as it will go, and we are now in the realm of faith.

In *Friends Journal* of January 1983, I wrote *The Case Against Boycotts*. There I argued all the usual positions: that sanctions against South Africa will bring misery, even death, to the poor; that they are a form of war; that they do not work, and so on and on and on. These reasons, I believe, are all true, and further, that if truly effective sanctions *could* be achieved, they would be the most disastrous thing that could happen to Africa in this century, drought and war not excluded.

But the real reason I oppose sanctions is that they are not a moral way to live. The society we create is how we create it. Threat is not consonant with love.

Chapter 19

Pacifism

In 1979, a *New Republic* writer (Chapman) decried what he saw as "the lost pacifism of American Quakers" and their "alliance with any number of explicitly violent movements (in third-world countries), making only the mildest demurrals about the means such movements employ."

This article and similar criticisms both within and without the Society of Friends led to the issuance of two important statements. The first, by Stephen Cary, Chairperson of the American Friends Service Committee (AFSC), stated:

> But it is not enough to be against armed violence. We believe, together with the profound Quaker spiritual leader, Lucretia Mott, that the world cries out not only for peace but for the achievement of social justice.

The AFSC became more explicit in a statement approved by its Board of Directors on January 24, 1981, in which it declared:

> Violence inevitably accompanies injustice, however, and the peace for which we strive will not reign while patterns of inequity and oppression continue. In each area of struggle there are indigenous people and groups who work for the same broad goals we seek, but few sustain a

> principled refusal to use violence to advance their cause . . .
>
> Although we see the frequently gross disparity between violence of the powerful as against violence of those seeking to end their own oppression -- although we yearn for an end to galling exploitation -- we cannot endorse the use of violence . . .

The statement goes on to declare that while the AFSC opposes violence for any end, it will not abandon its nurture of all groups in the Third World who oppose oppression, even though they may themselves opt for violence.

I believe Chapman's article, Steve Cary's reply, and the AFSC policy statement helped delineate the position of Friends; I was also encouraged to see an unequivocal endorsement of nonviolence by the AFSC. But I remain troubled by the phrase "indigenous people and groups who work for the same broad goals we seek," for I believe they are the Molochs to which Jim Corbett referred in the Foreword.

Whatever goals these groups may verbalize, they believe in achieving them by violence. If the past is guide, they will turn out not to be the goals of the masses at all. Hence they can be enforced only by violence. History - ancient, medieval, and what is going on right now - tell us that coercive governments always oppress, no matter what they say in advance and no matter how they behave when they first take power. Robespierre and Stalin are the arch prototypes, but other historical examples abound. I believe that goals of Friends should not be a specific form of government but a way of behaving under any government and a way of behaving to change a government.

I believe the proposition that "violence inevitably accompanies injustice" is not only historically untrue; it is an oblique abandonment of pacifism. There have been many,

many, many instances in history when injustices were not met by violence. Matthew Melko has co-authored two books, listed in the bibliography, describing long periods of peace in both the ancient and modern worlds, periods not always known for their justice. There have also been peaceful ways to resolve injustices, as I have shown in chapter 11, which tells how Japanese and European peasants dismantled feudalism.

Both the Left and the Right have their own stereotypes of society created by untruths or distorted reasoning. In general, Friends have not succumbed to those of the Right. But if we adopt those of the Left, we are putting together the Great Jig-Saw Puzzle of the Left. Each piece is colored by the overall ideology. When they are finally assembled, and only one remains, it is big and red, and it says WAR. If Friends try to substitute a blue one labeled PEACE, we find only that it will not fit.

When the specific ends become more important than the means to achieve them, so that we ally ourselves with groups according to their ends rather than according to their means, then we risk abandoning our initiating and sustaining principles.

What does pacifism mean? It means abhorrence of war, unwillingness to participate in war under any circumstances, and denial that war will ever bring about social justice.

Chapter 20

What Can One Person Do?

After Kenya, I was in a box. I had spent years studying economic planning, only to conclude that planning made it easier for the rich to extort from the poor. Both personal observations and studies of history had undermined my faith that élitist governments, whether socialist or not, would help the poor. But many years earlier, when I received my doctorate, I had decided to use my skills to help humankind. Now those skills seemed useless. What to do?

I thought back on Art Mosher, when he was Director of the Agricultural Development Council. Art didn't tell farmers what seed they should use. Visiting a third-world village, he would pick out the farmer producing the best seed locally; he would buy some and hire others to plant it. Then he would leave town. The rest - he knew - they could figure out for themselves. Later on, he would send a post card. "Why did you send that?" the farmers would ask when next they saw him; "you know we can't read." "How can I help you improve your crops if you can't read?" Art would counter, again leaving the rest to them.

I thought of George Butler. In 1973, George was the sole American in a project in Western Province, Kenya, called Partnership for Productivity. PfP was the brainchild of David Scull of Langley Hill Meeting in Virginia, to which Robin and I used to belong. David, who had a small business of his own, wanted to make modern management practices available to tiny businesses in the Third World. He had hired George as field specialist.

When Robin and I visited George, he took us to his clients. George did not have an agenda, and he never gave advice. He would simply ask, "How are things going?" When the baker said he needed a larger oven, George asked him whether he had been to the bank. Only if the baker seemed interested would George explain how to get a loan. If the shirtmaker complained that his family was spending the money he needed for cloth, George would ask him whether he kept separate accounts for the business and the household. If the shirtmaker asked how to do that, George might suggest two jars: business money in one, family money in the other. If that seemed sensible, the shirtmaker would do it; if it didn't, he wouldn't.

I thought about Jimmie Yen, a Chinese who, while a graduate student at Yale during World War I, was sent to France to help organize Chinese trenchdiggers. Homesick, the illiterate workers asked him to write letters to their families. This he did, but one day he said he would do it no more. Instead, he would teach them to write.

Upon his return to China, Jimmie continued his literacy program, but he combined it with village and agricultural development. He called it "rural reconstruction," the closest English equivalent to the Chinese expression. When the communists took power in 1949, Jimmie moved to Taiwan. There Chiang Kai-shek put him in charge of land reform.

Jimmie went to the United States, met President Truman, and with American help he formed the Joint Commission for Rural Reconstruction. Pearl Buck (1959) wrote a book about Jimmie; he appears in major textbooks on the Far East; and he has been featured in the *Reader's Digest* more than once.

President Magsaysay of the Philippines was so impressed by Jimmie's work that he offered him land in the Philippines, where the International Institute of Rural

Reconstruction (IIRR) grew. Its program has expanded into many countries, but each national agency works quietly with villagers, improving agriculture, village government, health, and cultural expression, never imposing itself, never taking a political stand, always fitting in with what villagers perceive as their needs.

What, in general, can I say about Art, George, and Jimmie? Only that they were all helping the poor to empower themselves. Nothing they have done will force radical change in our generation. But - together with thousands of other Arts, Georges, and Jimmies - they will change society a century from now. There are hundreds of organizations out there, and virtually any skill that anyone has in the industrial world can be put to work.

From Art, George, and Jimmie I learned that we must have faith in the inner resources of human beings. These three, and others like them, even influenced my mode of teaching in the university. I no longer give lectures, no longer dispense "answers," but I do ask questions. For the same reason, when Friends ask me "what can one Friend do," I cannot answer for any "one Friend" other than myself. But let's try a few general thoughts anyway.

Before turning to the positives, let us review the negatives. First, let us avoid any belief in land reform by grace, or government by champion, as in Algeria or China or Cuba or El Salvador or Nicaragua or the Soviet Union or Tanzania. Second, let us avoid the trap that justice for the poor will come about by war or indeed has come about by war. War with victory concentrates power, which abuses the peasant. Third, let us accept that genuine reform will not happen overnight. We must be persistent but patient.

Foremost among the positives, let us believe in the peasant, help him or her to gain the strength from which to bargain. If we are farmers, doctors, teachers, engineers, lawyers, business managers, mechanics, social workers, or have any other skill, there are organizations through which we can work.

Norman Illsley, a Quaker, started a sustained career in the Third World by turning Volkswagen engines into hand tractors. Jack Urner, another Quaker, has made his career consulting abroad, on economic development, while his wife, Carol Reilly Urner, has found ways to help rural and urban poor wherever in the Third World they have lived. She helps locate projects for the Friends World Committee on Consultation, whose "Right Sharing" program now operates in about twenty countries. Juan Pascoe, a Mexican Quaker, served with the United Nations. In Kenya, my wife Robin worked with the American Women's Association to bring resources to poor communities. Mac McBane, a Presbyterian missionary, trained mechanics in a small school in Pakistan. My son Ken, fresh out of college, is working with IIRR in the Philippines right now, helping farmers claim their rights under the land reform law.

In South Africa, Quakers help their black compatriots negotiate the maze of laws, so they can make the best of unfair courts and bureaucracy. Working with the AFSC, Susan Gunn helped nomads in Mali to form permanent settlements when their population exceeded the capacity of the land. Also with the AFSC, Bob Ledogar helped families in the urban slums of Zambia. When a tactical retreat became necessary, Friends have helped the persecuted to escape, through Sanctuary on the Mexican border. Yet these are only among the people and projects that I know. How many more there must be that I do not know!

We might help village moneylenders gain greater access to credit, tying their operations into modern banks. We might assist health, sanitation, and education. We might promote ways by which various classes in village societies learn to trust each other, with improved methods of business management. We might tell peasants of new ways in agriculture that have been successful elsewhere, always remembering, however, that agriculture is local-specific and the peasant is the best judge of what will work locally. We must take a low profile in all of these, fitting in, neither directing nor helping an élitist government to direct.

If we can't participate in these activities ourselves, we can give money to the hundreds of organizations that do. I have now addressed the question of Chapter 9: "If there is to be no champion, then what is the role for Quakers?" But I have not answered it for you or you.

Helping in a simple way is like voting. One vote won't win the election, yet all votes together determine the destiny of a nation.

Chapter 21

The Journey Continues

The journey is not yet over. The "retirement" I now approach will be a gentle, relative shift. I will not stop teaching, so long as I am able, but I will do less of it, and I will work more on *The Horizon Society*.

Have I learned anything along the way? I list a few insights below. So long as I learn, they may be changed. Your insights may be different, and I will respect them. But if mine are of any use to others, then it has been worth my while to write this story of my odyssey.

First, what is right will probably work, and what is wrong will probably fail - often not right away, but usually in the long run.

Second, it is better to do good than to do nothing. But it is better to do nothing than to do harm.

Third, there is nothing wrong with being a champion, provided the champion does not steal the show from those championed, does not direct them, and does not patronize them. More often than not, however, the champion does.

Fourth, do not engage in a social protest whose success depends on its failure. "Well, it would be harmful if everyone did it, but if only a few do, it will be a strong protest."

Fifth, watch out for bandwagons. When the whole society, or even much of the Society of Friends, suddenly veers in one direction, then especially is the time to ask: "Is this correct?" Sometimes it is, but more often it is not.

Sixth, behind every social action should stand a principle. For those who favor sanctions on South Africa, the principle may be: "We must use our economic power to prevent others from doing harm." My principle is: "It is wrong for the rich to threaten with their wealth."

Seventh, if we deprecate our own society, we cloud our vision of peaceful change, for it is in our own civilization that that change has mostly occurred.

Eighth, social revolution comes slowly, not because we want it to, but because if we force it, it fails. Violence re-creates the society its perpetrators want to change, just with different power brokers.

Ninth, social change occurs by gradual increments in the strength of the poor, forged by the poor themselves, in thousands upon thousands of actions, none individually spectacular, but in the aggregate powerful.

A quotation from Arthur Schlesinger, Jr., comes to mind, which I commend to American society at large as well as more specially to the Society of Friends:

> History, by putting crisis into perspective, supplies the antidote to every generation's illusion that its own problems are uniquely oppressive.

Throughout my journey, I have believed in the rightness of plural societies, decentralization of power, widespread ownership of wealth, compromise and conflict resolution rather than violence, and in the slow growth of institutions to moderate all these things. Not that these institutions take precedence over economic justice, but that they are essential to it.

How, then, do we solve current oppression, peacefully and immediately? That question is so American, and so Quaker. I have mentioned a few ways in which we may try, but each person's path is peculiar unto that person. The only generality is that if we try to do it all at once, or if we even "know" all the steps to the goal, we will fail. But if we take a first step in harmony with the right direction, the way for the next will open.

Afterword

The Creative Tension in Being a Quaker Economist

by Kenneth Boulding

As another Quaker economist - a somewhat rare breed - I have read Jack Powelson's "personal journey" with great interest and sympathy. It is indeed a modern version of the classic Quaker journal which brings out dramatically something I have felt in my own life, the "creative tension" between two cultures. One is the intimate, highly personal but demanding culture of the Society of Friends, with its roots in the Judeo-Christian phylum, as Teilhard de Chardin called it, as it evolves through recorded history. The other is that of the professional economics community, also with deep roots in Christian Europe, but branching out from the eighteenth-century Enlightenment with its dominating emphasis on the search for truth, that is, images in the mind which correspond to some real world.

These two cultures intersect, at times tortuously, as Jack Powelson has found out. The Quaker movement resisted domination by authority and insisted on testing Truth through personal experience. "This I knew experimentally," said George Fox. "You will say Christ saith this and the Apostles say this, but what can'st Thou say?" asked Margaret Fell. But the Quaker search for Truth also corresponded to the four moral principles around which the scientific community has been built: (1) CURIOSITY: what is the world really like? (2) VERACITY: truth-telling, and eschewing of lies. (3) TESTING: which may take many forms. (4) PERSUASION BY EVIDENCE: not by threat or coercion.

These value pillars are fundamental to both the scientific community and the Society of Friends. It is not surprising, therefore, that Quakers made a disproportionate contribution to the scientific revolution and also to the social and technical revolutions of the eighteenth and early nineteenth centuries: John Dalton, the founder of modern chemistry; Abram Darby, who discovered how to smelt iron with coal; John Gurney and the Lloyd family, innovators in banking, all were Quakers. The first railroad, the Stockton and Darlington, was financed by Quakers. Quakers set fixed prices because bargaining - saying one would sell for one price and settling for another - compromised veracity. *It should also follow that Quakers would want to understand social revolution today through the eyes of scientific economists as well as religious seekers.*

Curiously enough, I know of no Quaker economist before the twentieth century. Quakers were slow in entering higher education and academic life. Until about 1850, Quakers might not attend Oxford and Cambridge, since these were preserves of the Church of England. Even in America, Quakers were late in embracing higher education. Haverford College was founded in 1834, nearly 200 years after Harvard. Perhaps Friends' attitude reflected George Fox's insight that "one did not have to be bred at Oxford and Cambridge to be a minister of the gospel."

Despite the overlap between the Quaker and the scientific culture, tensions still arise. The main source, I suspect, is that the Quaker culture is intensely personal and small scale, both in the meeting for worship, which is the core of Quaker experience, and in the concerns for "mending the world," which arise out of it. Partly these concerns require withdrawal from activities regarded as evil, such as lying, cheating, fighting, killing, and obedience to illegitimate authority. Partly they involve reaching out to people in trouble and helping them, no matter who they are, with "implacable love."

As part of the scientific community, however, economists tend not to be personal but to view the world as a total system. I once defined economics as the study of how the world was organized through exchange and through one-way transfers by such things as taxation and grants. Exchange demands a minimum framework of personal relationships: courtesy, trust, and reputation. When we trade with a machine, such as a soft-drink vendor, however, the relationship is not deep, even though people have been known to kick a machine that didn't come through when the money was paid in.

Another source of conflict in being both a Quaker and a scientist arises from the fact that what is true in the individual experience is often not true for the system as a whole. An individual can easily spend more than is received and so run down his or her money stock. But other people get what the individual spends, so the system has lost no money. The "echo effects" - A does something to B, B does something to C, C to D, D to E, and so on, all around the system, often back to A again - are frequently surprising. Often what we do to help people actually hurts them and what we do to hurt them sometimes helps them.

Mending the world, therefore, is by no means easy. Good will is not enough. There must be good understanding as well. Somehow we have to develop a humility that is not paralyzing. Sometimes we have to act out of ignorance, but it is never right to act out of unnecessary ignorance.

This, I believe, is the message Jack Powelson has tried to convey. It is a very important one. We must recognize that the old distinctions between Right and Left have become blurred and no longer correspond to any simple bad-good scale. The time is ripe for new inquiries into which actions make for human betterment and which do not. A careful reading of *Facing Social Revolution* can be a good beginning for these new inquiries.

References

Barton, Clifton, 1974:
Problems and Prospects of Small Industries in the Republic of Vietnam, Saigon, Industrial Development Bank of Saigon, December.

Berger, Peter, 1986:
Fifty Propositions about Prosperity, Equality, and Liberty, New York, Basic Books. See Lester Thurow's review of this book in *New York Times Book Review*, 9/7/86.

Berryman, Phillip, 1983:
What's Wrong in Central America, and What to Do About It, Revised edition, Philadelphia, Pa., American Friends Service Committee.

Blum, Jerome, 1978:
The End of the Old Order in Rural Europe, Princeton, NJ, Princeton University Press.

Brayshaw, A. Neave, 1953:
The Quakers: Their Story and Message, London, Friends Home Service Committee.

Buck, Pearl, 1959:
Tell the People: Talks with James Yen About the Mass Education Movment, New York, International Institute of Rural Reconstruction.

Chapman, Stephen, 1979:
"Shot from Guns: The Lost Pacifism of American Quakers," *The New Republic*, June 9.

Conquest, Robert, 1986:
The Harvest of Sorrow: Soviet Collectivization and the Terror- Famine, New York, Oxford University Press.

Friends Committee on National Legislation, 1982:
Washington Newsletter, Washington, D.C.

Gregg, Pauline, 1961:
Free-Born John: A Biography of John Lilburne, London, George G. Harrap and Co., reprinted, 1974, in Westport, CT, by Greenwood Press.

Harden, Blaine, 1986:
"Watch 'The Africans' With the Sound Turned Off," *Washington Post Weekly*, October 20.

IADB = Inter-American Development Bank, 1984:
Economic and Social Progress in Latin America, Washington DC.

Kriedte, Peter, 1983:
Peasants, Landlords, and Merchant Capitalists: Europe and the World Economy, 1500-1800, New York, Cambridge University Press (translation from a German work of 1980).

Lambton, Ann, 1953:
Landlord and Peasant in Persia: A Study of Land Tenure and Land Revenue Administration, New York, Oxford University Press.

Lele, Uma, 1972:
"Role of Credit and Marketing Functions in Agricultural Development," mimeographed paper presented at International Economic Association Conference on "Agriculture in the Development of Low Income Countries," Bad Godesberg, Germany, August 26-September 4.

Melko, Matthew, and Weigel, Richard D., 1981:
Peace in the Ancient World, Jefferson, N.C., McFarland & Co.

Melko, Matthew, and Hord, John, 1984:
Peace in the Western World, Jefferson, N.C., McFarland & Co.

NYT = *New York Times*.

Penn, William (see Tolles and Alderfer 1957).

Powelson, Jack, 1966:
"They Saw and were Broadened," *Friends Journal*, June.

Powelson, John P., and Stock, Richard, 1987:
The Peasant Betrayed: Agriculture and Land Reform in the Third World, Boston, Oelgeschlager Gunn and Hain, for the Lincoln Institute of Land Policy.

Powelson, John P., 1987:
The Story of Land: A World History of Land Tenure and Agrarian Reform, Boston, Oelgeschlager Gunn and Hain, for the Lincoln Institute of Land Policy.

Powelson, John P., 1964:
Latin America: Today's Economic and Social Revolution, New York, McGraw-Hill.

Powelson, John P., 1964:
"The Land Grabbers of Cali," *The Reporter*, January.

Reynolds, Lloyd G., 1975:
Agriculture in Development Theory, New Haven, CT, Yale University Press.

Robertson, Priscilla, 1952:
Revolutions of 1848: A Social History, Princeton, NJ, Princeton University Press.

Rosenn, Keith S., 1984:
"Brazil's Legal Culture: The Jeito Revisited," *Florida International Law Journal*, vol. 1, no. 1, Fall.

Russell, Elbert, 1979:
The History of Quakerism, Richmond IN, Friends United Press.

Schlesigner, Arthur M., Jr., 1986:
"The Challenge of Change," *New York Times Magazine*, July 27.

Tolles, Frederick B.and Alderfer, eds., 1957:
The Witness of William Penn, New York, Macmillan. (The quotation at the end of chapter 18 is on page 188).

USDC = United States Department of Commerce, 1974, 1986:
Statistical Abstract of the United States, Washington DC.

Index